The Truth Will Set You Free

For work has no other aim
Than getting knowledge of truth
When that comes, work is put away—
The flower blooms for the fruit
When the fruit comes, the flower withers
                    KABIR

The Truth Will Set You Free

Svāmi Pūrṇá

New Age Books

ISBN: 978-81-7822-314-8

First Indian Edition: Delhi, 2008

© Adhyatmik Foundation, Inc 1987

Published by
NEW AGE BOOKS
A-44 Naraina Phase-I
New Delhi-110 028 (INDIA)
Email: nab@vsnl.in
Website: www.newagebooksindia.com

Printed in India
at Shri Jainendra Press
A-45 Naraina Phase-I, New Delhi-110 028

Contents

The Truth is your birthright:
no one can take it from you.

SVĀMI PŪRṆĀ

1

The Truth will Set you Free

For work has no other aim
Than getting knowledge of truth
When that comes, work is put away –
The flower blooms for the fruit
When the fruit comes, the flower withers

KABIR

Two birds of identical appearance come to rest in a tree full of ripe, deliciously tempting fruit. One of the birds, Jivatman, tastes the fruit and finds it so enthralling he cannot stop eating. He forgets the presence of his companion bird, Paramatman, who sits quietly on a branch and watches, unperturbed and content. Paramatman is not tempted by the fruit.

The season changes and the fruit is no more. Frantic with hunger and sorrow, Jivatman flies from tree to tree in search of the fruit. He cannot live without it. His faithful friend accompanies him, patiently awaiting the return of Jivatman's sanity. He understands the delusion of attachment and knows that once Jivatman remembers his true identity and sees his friend, Paramatman, as his own self, he will be able to live without the fruit. He will be free from attachment, sorrow, pain or reliance upon any tree.

This story from the *Upanishads* illustrates the illusion of duality which separates the individual soul from the Real Self. The tree symbolizes the physical body. Jivatman, the personality, is the enjoyer who becomes increasingly involved with sensations and external activities, thereby losing identity with his true self. Jivatman is caught in the web of illusion and has forgotten the external reality which is his friend, Paramatman. He will suffer through the cycle of birth,

1

death and innumerable incarnations – always obsessed with the fruit – until the key to Reality is realized.

As one focuses attention upon the development of inner strength, higher growth begins to unfold. One learns to discriminate between positive and negative influences within oneself and the environment. This provides the ability to choose growth-enhancing activities and associations. With awareness comes choice. Ignorance affords no such freedom. To achieve awareness, one must listen inwardly and concentrate the will-power, which is a combination of aspiration and energy, upon the goal of seeing beyond the immediate and apparent. Self-observation is the key. Ultimately, the individual holds responsibility for growth. If the individual is the cause of separation, the individual is also the driving force for re-integration.

This is not easy work. Humans are not trained in self-observation. This is where the teacher – guru – master comes in. Self-observation is the most important tool of evolution; but only one who has achieved, has finished the work, can instruct in proper implementation. One must look to someone who has travelled the path and can see the traps, someone who represents the evolution one seeks to achieve.

The teacher is not an extension of personality or identity, except in the highest philosophical sense, as Paramatman is related to Jivatman. To say, "My Teacher . . . " or "I am the disciple of . . . " in a possessive and ego-defining way is a disservice to both teacher and student. The quest is the important thing. Travelling the path to inner growth is not like joining a club; the guru is not the entertainer, the disciple is not the audience. This unfortunate manifestation of false spiritual aspiration indicates that one is still chasing that elusive fruit. When external identification ends and one sees we are all manifestations of the same energy expressed in varying ways, the differentiation between illusion and truth becomes clearer.

A guru is someone who teaches through example . . . a reflection of what one wishes to become. Concentrate upon the guru as if looking into your highest Self. You, Jivatman, recognize in the mirror of the guru your own potential,

Paramatman. As this vision is internalized and strengthened with contemplation and meditation and one-pointed determination, it expands into insight which spills out into your external activities. You become aware that your actions in the world are the physical manifestations of your level of spiritual growth. One's level of awareness is constantly expressed in thoughts, gestures and interaction with the environment.

Fortunate is he who meets a God-realized being: blessed is he who is able to learn from that being. You may say your master is Jesus Christ, Buddha, Krishna or simply the Life Force, God. But can you see the light of Christ? Do you have the capacity to receive His teachings? Can you perceive the sound of Krishna? If you are not attuned to your guru and can neither hear nor see what is given, you delude yourself in believing you are a follower of that being. Of course, following the examples and teachings of the guru diligently and with all your heart will eventually result in attunement. The point is that to communicate with God is not an ordinary ability. You must uplift yourself to communicate.

There are valuable lessons to be learned by the perceptive seeker in every aspect and corner of life. There is a descending chain of evolved beings which come to earth from time to time, but one can also learn from nature. Mountains represent those qualities of firmness and stability one must acquire to progress spiritually. Rivers express fluidity and flexibility; trees illustrate forebearance; and the sun teaches us to give without exception or prejudice – it just shines, for everyone and everything. Who can doubt the unfathomable power of oceans to affect our consciousness? Or the moon, constant and reliable, yet ever moving throughout her phases? The clarity of an energy-filled sky and the turbulance of weather systems which come from 'out of the blue' are examples and reminders of our own mental systems . . . and the volatility of thought.

A sage of ancient India, Dattatreya, is said to have been taught by twenty-four gurus. By observing a dog, he learned loyalty, alertness and mindfulness; from a prostitute he observed the quality of non-attachment and unconcern; a watercarrier balancing five pitchers at once upon her head while walking, talking, gesticulating and laughing, yet never upsetting the balance, taught him to be aware. No matter what actions his body and mind undertook, he was ever aware of his true nature, Paramatman.

The human being is indocrinated from birth to focus on the external, physical aspects of life. We are taught to objectify the world and its inhabitants and even God. People, things, places and even feelings – love, hate, anger – are seen as tools, pieces to move around as in a child's game. We develop material strategies and learn to manipulate ourselves and others to get as much as we can of the 'fruit'. This attitude is the antithesis of true awareness of our position in life. We are here to evolve, learn, grow, not to play a game. In truth, there is no other game than God's, and in that game He is the only player.

The correct attitude toward God has been captured beautifully by Guru Nanak in the following stanza from the *Guru Granth*:

> Who knows Your mystery, but You alone –
> Who cannot but accept You?
> Unable to comprehend Your play –
> I can but surrender myself at Your feet.

The entire creation is God's play. One cannot judge or comprehend it, but one can fulfil one's own potential, thereby playing a role in God's play. Energy is everywhere and everything is energy; our challenge is to discover the appropriate applications of life force. Everything has purpose and meaning and a definite function and role within the play of the highest reality. We must not, therefore, waste our own precious energy, nor should we discount the importance of other life forms to the totality of God's scheme. Even a mosquito, that often maligned insect, fulfils some purpose. It is a tiny recycler, besides providing food for frogs and snakes. Since it lays its eggs in dirt, and the energy from the dirt is absorbed during gestation, it is actually using filth in a positive way, thereby rendering it less harmful and preventing some diseases. And the mosquito is a form of consciousness, or energy; to say all mosquitoes must be removed from the earth is not enlightened behaviour. It is unwise to reject anything. The more fully we develop, the more clearly we recognize this truth.

All matter is in a state of change. Creation, growth and eventual disintegration are the interacting rules of nature. Physical immortality is a misconception and a false goal. It is, again, attachment to the fruit. One day, each human body will cease to be of use and will have to be returned to nature's bank from which it was borrowed. Mother Nature has lent us the five elements – earth, fire, water, air and space – entrusting us with the responsibility to use them wisely until the loan is due for repayment. It is sad when after seventy or eighty years we realize we could have invested more wisely. It is all too easy to forget the sanctity of God's temple, the physical body, until irreparable damage has been done. In ignorance, we search for sensual pleasure until we find ourselves at the stage of complete disaster. We misuse the body by doting upon negativity, wrong food, wasteful conversation, associations which take us away from our higher goals. Why should we feel shock when the body fails us? It would seem the natural progression. Non-attachment to body does not mean neglect of health. The physical body is a vehicle for growth-through-action in life, and must be cared for with at least the same awareness, concern and attention to detail many of us give our cars. The body is to be used, not preserved. But it can be tuned, overhauled and cleansed through discipline and understanding of its purpose.

Disease illustrates disharmony between body, mind and spirit and can give valuable clues to changes that need to be made in lifestyle and thought. Our emotions and mental distortions reflect in physical form as disease symptoms; aches, pains and tensions are accumulations of blocked or misspent energy. With detachment from body-consciousness and awareness of a true Self which is eternal and profoundly powerful, one can read the clues and correct the maladjustment. Prevention, of course, is best. Some who have illusions about the role of the body seek every artificial means to promote

5

outer attractiveness and the appearance of health, projecting a pleasing veneer over a frequently diseased and decrepit interior. In delusion they treat the body as a treasured possession, becoming obsessed with its preservation. Others seek perpetual youth and immortality in rituals and religious practices which do little to uplift them spiritually. It is true that advanced yogis are able to attain a state of health and physical power far beyond the bounds of ordinary biology, even remaining youthful to a very advanced age. But rather than a form of body-consciousness, this achievement of physical perfection is a side effect, or a tool, of total commitment to spiritual realization and dedication to God's play.

Miracles are like fool's gold. The student who insists the guru prove himself with demonstrations of the miraculous is caught in the same illusion as the bird flying from tree to tree in search of fruit. Such a student will learn nothing, but will move from guru to guru trying to find the one who does the most impressive tricks. That is entertainment. Real gold lies hidden within the heart of the serious spiritual seeker. Miraculous powers may exist, but a wise being has no need to show off. Wisdom precludes sensationalism. There is no need. One must look to the motivation.

There is a legend about Lord Shiva to illustrate the uselessness of miracles. In response to great austerities by a demon, the Great God, Shiva, offered a boon. "What do you want of me, that you have worked so hard to please me?" asked Shiva in benevolence. The demon replied, "When I put my hand on the head of a person, he should immediately be burned to ashes." Lord Shiva granted the somewhat gruesome request, delighting the demon, who answered, "All right, first you!" A shocked Shiva resorted to flight as the demon tried to touch his head. The demon's motivation had not been to please the Lord but to gain the affections of Shiva's consort, Parvati. As this little drama unfolded, another divine manifestation, Lord Vishnu, watched with interest. It was quite a sight, Shiva running here and there, the demon in hot pursuit, hand poised to incinerate the God of Destruction. Vishnu decided to intervene and, changing himself into the form of Parvati, confronted the demon in a seductive manner. "Really," she said, "why bother chasing after Shiva when I am willing to come to you? You are so attractive, there is no need to destroy Shiva." This pleased the vanity of the demon who approached Parvati with demonic lust. "No . . . wait, please," she halted him. "Whenever Shiva comes to me, he performs this wonderful dance first." "But I cannot dance," said the demon dejectedly. "Never mind, I will show you," replied Parvati, and she began to teach him the movements of the Tandava, which involves placing one hand upon the head! So the demon danced . . . He danced the dance of destruction with all his heart and soul, and a small pile of ashes at the feet of Parvati was all that remained of him. In the meantime, Shiva had watched the spectacle from behind a clump of bushes. The danger over, He ventured forth to meet the admonishing gaze of Vishnu, now Himself again. "Granting boons to demons, indeed!" reminded Vishnu.

Shiva may have demonstrated His powers with no other motivation than love, even toward a demon, but the result was disaster. It is a mistake to associate any kind of sensationalism with Divinity. The performance of miracles does not gauge the calibre of spiritual awareness in God or guru. Jesus Christ is often proclaimed a Divine Being because He healed the sick. It is *because* He was a Divine Being that He was able to heal the sick. His teachings and qualities of non-attachment, love, kindness and mercy showed Him to be a High Being, not merely a performer of fantastic spectacles.

It is unfortunate that religious dogma so often clutters and confuses the truth of spiritual teachings. Symbolism as well as incorrect translation and interpretation have lowered the level of many of the world's religious organisations. Certainly, it is more important to concentrate on the *teachings* of the guru, of Christ, for instance, than to focus on the dogma of a religious sect, which is often politically orientated and confused. What is the real spiritual significance of the details of how, when or where Christ died? The important gift of Christ would seem to be His teachings; after all, He was given the choice to renounce them and He chose crucifixion instead. That is the real lesson

. . . He would not renounce, which shows how crucial the maintenance and propagation of His sacred teachings were to Him. The idea that He died for your sins, the story of the immaculate conception or the resurrection and all the dogma which originated not from Him but from later fathers of the church merely obscure the real purpose of Christ's existence on earth.

The Koran is a similar case of manipulation. Mohammed, the messenger of God, used to receive inspiration from God while in the highest state of consciousness. The collected records of these inspirations form the Koran. But at a later date, someone thought it prudent to amend and modify the original. The result differs significantly from the records of the Prophet. The Day of Judgement, for instance, is said to be the day when God will destroy all 'infidels'. Only Muslims will be allowed to live. Now, one must consider the meaning of the word 'Muslim': 'One who has surrendered to God'. Could this be a local God? Is God not universal? How about the Aborigine or Eskimo who surrenders to God? And what happens to the man in Persia or Saudi Arabia or the Soviet Union who calls himself a Muslim, but has never surrendered to God? Many other religions have similar man-made misrepresentations that have nothing to do with spiritual growth. They are, in fact, anti-evolution. It is easy to distort the Truth, for so few are willing to stop chasing illusion, listen for a moment, wonder about the essence of God, of Reality, and resist the urge to flutter from tree to tree in search of delicious fruit.

If God is all-mighty, all-knowing and all-pervading, then God is within you, within me, within the smallest seed of the tiniest twig that will, with nourishment and love, grow to be a glorious, deliciously fruited tree. But this fruit will be Truth . . . and this truth will set you free.

2

Maya's Play

*After all our studies we only acquire
that which we put into practice*

GOETHE

Appearances matter. This is, of course, a play on words. Appearances are often illusions; matter is Maya. In a more profound sense, however, an individual's growth will reflect in his outward appearance. It is important that one create a positive impression, which is the natural outcome of inner positivity. This cannot be assumed like a mask; if it is not a true reflection of inner growth, it is useless. A person who merely talks of action is not in reality a person of action. In the same vein, the wearing of the saffron robe does not ensure enlightenment or sainthood.

Many people speak about personal qualities which they do not actually possess, as if trying to project an image on a screen outside of themselves. They hope that others will believe what appears there rather than what is really going on inside. It is very tempting to talk, talk, talk . . . and talk is cheap. In a spiritual sense these people are fooling no one but themselves. Anyone with 'eyes to see' can see right through them to the truth within. We should be living examples of our convictions. It is of no import whatsoever to broadcast, "I am this . . . I am that . . . " It is a valueless pastime. For instance, concerning growth. Suppose you were very bad in the past – a really rotten person – and you are now transformed; your personality is totally different; you have become kind and gentle towards people. Do you actually think no one will notice unless you tell them? People will come to know your quality by your action, not by your words.

Of course, it is tempting to talk and to be caught in Maya's web. During sadhana, for example, perhaps you look into the mirror daily hoping that the third eye is opening. You go around telling others about your new feelings and experiences and the details of your sadhana. You ask them if they can see your third eye. They respond by seeing you as a fanatic and a fool! In this way you make a mockery of yourself and your efforts to grow, not to mention your guru. There is no need to advertise. If you change your personality and behaviour, people will notice. The diamond does not have to proclaim its value with a price ticket. Its value shines out for itself through its quality.

Growth is the most precious entity one can acquire in life. At the same time it can be quite costly. One must pay for growth by giving up conditions of mind which prevent growth. This is a very high price for most. Apparently illusion (Maya) is a very dear thing to many people, for they cling to it until death rather than make the exchange that could guarantee *life*. They choose to hang their fates on the wheel of fortune and they suffer the repetition of endless deaths under the karmic law of cause and effect.

Whatever life situations you are involved in materially, you must be careful not to be blinded by the drama of Maya. It is too easy to see only the apparent, fleeting images of the senses and to miss the entire theme and essence of life. The physical senses can only perceive material and sensual experiences. They are limited as organs of spiritual perception. As one's consciousness grows, these organs of material perception are purified and sensitized to a higher tone or frequency of vibration. They become transformed. Maya is thereby defeated. Her false images are disintegrated, and she loses her ability to sway your mind or cloud your vision of life. Such growth can only happen when one is not blinded by the ornaments of Maya.

Let us not forget the mythological Narcissus who was so taken by his own physical perfection that he was unable to receive the love of the wood-nymph who adored him. He stagnated and died spiritually. He was hypnotized by a beautiful image reflected to him as he stared, forever, into a cold pool of water. Similarly, many lives are filled with emptiness as human beings fix their attention on surface appearances and neglect the deeper truths and objectives of their lives. There are innumerable distractions, petty problems and seductive desires encountered throughout any individual's lifetime. They are all part of Maya's Magical Picture Show – a trap to prevent one's growth out of infantile fantasies and into the resplendent consciousness that is never rewarded to those whose resistance is weak.

Sometimes these obstacles to growth come from without; at other times they are produced by the entity itself, springing from the dark well of past karma and samskara. This is not simply a barrage of evil coming to attack and destroy. It is, rather, a challenge and an opportunity for growth. One is fortunate to be presented with such chances in life to overcome the lower desires and feelings, and to transform oneself into a higher being than one was at birth. There is the choice to wallow in childish feelings of helplessness or to use the tools of meditation and contemplation, thereby developing clarity of mind and the ability to see through Maya's varied masks. When one has, in this manner, come to know the God within, one will be master of Maya rather than her servant. Certain behaviour will be out of the question – will seem totally inappropriate. God does not imitate the fool, does not act like a demon. It would certainly be ungodly behaviour within this state of consciousness to envy, lust, revel or lament over the ornaments of Maya. At this point one has reached a state of non-attachment and is therefore unaffected by the delusions and fancies which afflict those who think they are taking the 'easy' road of instant gratification.

What is often termed 'love' can be the darkest, most mysterious and destructive emotion. True love, however, is an implement of evolution as in Bhakti Yoga, the path of devotion. All too often, lower physical manifestations – such as lust, greed, and the desire for power – are misinterpreted as love. Sometimes, when one is unable to receive the affection which is craved, one turns to fantasies. The imagination creates events to be experienced as is desired, by manipulating and degrading others for selfish gratification, in a dream or hallucinatory state. When energy is used in this way, it promotes the delusion that one is getting what is desired. In reality, though, what is happening is the creation of an obsession based on unreality. If continued, this can lead to behaviour which is extremely unsuitable to the reality of the situation – it can also produce insanity. The responsibility for such fantasies belongs solely to the fantasy-maker. This perverse waste of energy and emotion is totally destructive and dangerous, allowing for repeated experience of unreality.

Love is pure. It is a selfless attitude of devotion to the unfolding and blossoming of Truth. Through love one can manifest to a higher level. Human beings need to love and to be loved. They also need to transform selfish love into selfless love. It is through such transmutation of lower urges into higher longing that one is able to attain more profound fulfilment and eventual enlightenment and liberation.

The thing to remember is: do not become trapped by any aspect of Maya. Even love of the guru can be a trap if it is distorted and negatively manifested. To be devoted, attentive and obedient – to implement the guru's teaching – is positive. The highest gift of love towards one's guru is total manifestation of his teachings. However, if one only responds on the physical level and does not grow through and beyond that attraction, one is demeaning the guru and wasting his precious time and effort. It is unhealthy to abuse the immaculate love of guru for disciple. guru – father; disciple – child. The guru is God's representative and should be respected as such unless he is considered to be just one of many who pretend to be guru but are fake. If one truly believes in the guru one must change the quality of love through determination and self-discipline. It is not easy to grow through Maya's tests. Consider this: the pressure of thousands of years can create a diamond out of a block of black coal, but only the fossil remains of the ancient dead.

Maya's traps do not disappear as one becomes more evolved. Until the final summit is reached, the chance to fall is always around the next bend. The story of Vishnu and his 'devotees' provides a good example of such tests.

Vishnu's disciple Narada was passing through a village and reflecting on the magnanimity of his Great Guru when he overheard a lot of commotion coming from a group of people gathered in one house. Moving closer he realized there was crying and a desperate plea for help. It was directed at Vishnu! Alarmed, he entered and heard the lament, "Oh Vishnu, why have you deserted us? You do not listen . . . you have no heart. How can you be so cruel? We long for you and you never come to us . . . " The rampant emotionalism influenced Narada. "I am touched by your feelings," he said. "I go now to Vishnu to tell him what I have seen and heard here." He went in anger and said to Vishnu, "He who called you the Lord of Compassion was a liar. You do not deserve such a name. Your devotees are crying in desperation and you do not hear them."

Vishnu listened to Narada's half-hour lecture then replied patiently, "I am always with my devotees. Nothing can stop me from being with them. Wherever they are, I am there. I do not live in caves or in yogis but in the hearts of my devotees. As I have promised, whenever a true devotee calls to me, I go to him."

"If that is so," said Narada, "why are you so cruel to them? They shed tears, they long for you." "If my devotees make one step towards me, I will move millions of steps towards them," said Vishnu. "Then let us go to Earth and see," replied Narada.

As they came down, just five miles from the gathering place of the devotees, Vishnu said, "Look, I have come millions of miles, can they not come five miles to see me?" So Narada went to the house to fetch the complaining ones and said to them jubilantly, "Dear brothers and sisters, you will be happy to hear that your beloved Vishnu is waiting for you just five miles away. All you have to do is follow me. How fortunate you are! Your prayers have been answered. Come, all of you, I will take you to the Lord."

Half of the people immediately rejected him; how to be sure that Vishnu was really waiting five miles away? They did not know this man; how could they just go off with him; he could be lying. Where is the evidence that Vishnu is there? The other half responded half-heartedly that there was no harm in seeing . . . so they set out with Narada to meet the Lord.

But at that moment Maya entered the picture in full force. She would test those souls who sought communion with God. That is her job; she shows who is suited and who is not. As the devotees approached the first mile, Maya shed coins everywhere along the ground. Half the people decided that maybe Vishnu was there and maybe not, but the first priority was to gather the coins. Narada warned them it was Maya's work and that the coins would turn to ashes once gathered and taken home. To no avail. At the second mile Maya's tool was silver. Again half the people stopped to collect it. Narada told them it was a test of their devotion to Vishnu, but they did not listen, blinded by greed. Maya took great delight in her games, casting gold around the three-mile point. Half the remaining followers were trapped. At four miles diamonds appeared and other precious stones too numerous to mention were scattered all over the ground. When at last Narada reached the Lord, he brought with him just *one* devotee who had not been swayed by illusion, but whose devotion had been strong enough to take him to meet Vishnu. The others who had complained with such emotion very quickly threw away the aim of their lives when temptation tested them. They were not fit. "Where are those millions who desired to see me?" asked Vishnu.

The process of growing through, as opposed to getting stuck at any point along the way, can be applied to all parts of life. As you interact in social situations, work, love and play, you affect other individuals. Your growth will reflect upon society in general. Do not forget that it is individuals who comprise any society – the quality of individual consciousness shapes the quality of the group. Inspire and be inspired by positivity wherever you can create or discover it!

In a marriage, as in a society, each partner inspires the other to higher growth, if the love is genuine. Sometimes, though, it is difficult to see behind the obstacles of Maya. You question your ability to achieve enlightenment. You wonder how on earth to develop a higher love. You want to discover God and the mystery of the cosmos but you feel inadequate . . . so why try? It is important to check negativity as soon as it begins to manifest. Constantly question yourself. With meditation, contemplation and humble devotion, answers will eventually come.

In the story of Ruskhan, the Muslim, there is a lovely example of physical love turning into spiritual love. Khan had seen a picture of Krishna and he was convinced that he had hopelessly fallen in love with the Beautiful Boy. However, after some time, he came into contact with the God; he learned to perceive Him beyond his own fantasies. By following Krishna's teachings and transforming his love from personal to universal, Khan became a saint. That is what is meant by growing through love; the essence of the love itself must change.

When you have made the effort of right thought, right speech and right action, you will change. The change may be a sudden revelation or it may be gradual. But it will happen, as you learn to see beyond Maya's temptations and tests. And your growth will affect and inspire others – you will be a positive energy-field, like a torch; others will want to know you and learn from your example. If they are caught in illusion, they may try to see you in a distorted way. However, if you maintain your integrity and positivity, you will offer them a chance to grow through their illusions and see you as you really are.

Admiration of the physical sort, as any filmstar or politician knows, is shallow – 'two a penny' is an apt colloquialism. Few, however, realize the danger hidden there. When one courts the admiration of others for selfish gain, through arousing the lower instincts of lust, greed or violence, one is responsible for the result. This can mean destruction of the 'public personality' who must accept the karma of thousands or even millions. The mass karma can affect him by blinding him with ego and distorting his values, dragging him down into an abyss of confusion and corruption. This is how selfishness and distortion end.

Distortion of values ultimately destroys the perpetrator, whether in power spheres, individual interaction or so-called 'love'. The difference between love of a merely physical kind and spiritual love is that the former causes degeneration, the latter engenders growth. On the spiritual path, one can purify one's own karma while helping others to evolve. Even power can be wielded with love and used as a tool for positivity. Look at the examples of Nehru and Sri Aurobindo. Both were educated to be politicians. However, Nehru is merely a personage found in history books, an ordinary human being who became a politician. Aurobindo became a High Being and a symbol of eternal, immortal love. Though he has left his body, Sri Aurobindo continues to inspire millions through his example and teaching.

The stages of growth vary. The attitude of a child is different from that of an adult. Take sweets, for example. Most children like sweets so much that, if parents do not intervene, they will eat them until they become sick. The 'grown-up' may also enjoy sweets, but he has learned to control his desire – he knows the healthy limit and adjusts accordingly. He has out-grown the desires of childhood. In like manner, we grow from gross to more subtle, finer stages of development. Sometimes a city like Hollywood seems enticing with its flash, glamour and 'tinsel'. The excitement is imagined, and when one has seen the reality, the initial illusion fades. One comes, eventually, 'to see' in a different way. When enough of the frills and shallow, outward aspects – the tinsel of life – have been observed and experienced, one hungers to see something beyond all that. This is the beginning of discrimination. Some are born with it, while others never develop it, even in old age. From childhood to the moment one leaves the physical body there are opportunities to discriminate and to grow. Un-fortunately, many choose to emulate children all their lives; never learning to be responsible for themselves, they spoil the work of others. It is sad that most get stuck in one form, one role, one lifestyle, one activity, one habitual manner of acting, one condition of mind, etc. for the entirety of their brief visits to earth. They are enmeshed in the manifold aspects of Maya – mistaking illusion for reality. We must strive always to grow through lower to higher realms of experience.

All sorts of misconceptions come about by association with duality. Since separating from the Source, humans have devised many beliefs to confuse themselves regarding their relation to God – to keep God outside of life. Humankind wants to 'do its own thing'. But a belief can be a hindrance to growth. It is a condition of mind, another of Maya's veils; she has many, and the expertise of her dance has mystified poets and philosophers through the ages – so adept is she at covering the Truth with this transparency or that. The vision is always slightly blurred and out of reach. What is life . . . what comes after? Some religions say that when you 'die' you end; others say that you 'pass on' to another place . . . and that you go 'home', wherever that is. In truth, one goes nowhere and comes from nowhere. According to an individual's levels of consciousness, the experience or perception of death may vary, but the reality – the Truth – does not change. A belief is a condition of mind, and all conditions must be broken if the Truth is to be seen.

There are many strange beliefs concerning the guru. For instance, that he will 'enlighten' the disciple by touching him on the head with his 'danda', like Cinderella's Fairy God-mother. Some expect their guru to act like Santa Claus and give whatever they ask . . . Some say they believe the guru is God – but they manifest their belief by ignoring his teaching and giving the poor guru a huge bundle of their bad karma, in return for his attention to their needs.

This is reminiscent of some people's distorted belief in the Christ: since he died for their sins, whatever sins they continue to perpetrate are absolved and forgotten with confession. So, they go on committing transgressions and saying how much they love the Saviour. Meanwhile, what is to be done with the Truth He taught? Is it to be ignored? Let us say that one believes the Christ to be beautiful, good, generous and pure, and that one considers humankind to be bad. Is humankind then doing its job by praising Jesus and disregarding His teachings? Is this His reward? Perhaps His sacrifice was in vain . . .? It is easy to take advantage of purity and kindness. It is convenient to create a belief to hide our laziness and help us forget our responsibility to grow. It is certainly easier to light a candle or offer words of praise than to dedicate oneself to self-discovery through meditation, contemplation, devotion and performance of right actions.

There are two abused phrases in the English language which many believe are capable of performing miracles: 'Thank you' and 'I am sorry' are merely aids to ending the responsibility either to return a kindness or to accept fault. They create illusion, i.e. "I have no need to feel obligated" . . . "What happened is too bad, but I am absolved from guilt."

Century upon century, many millions have proclaimed Christ as their Guru. The shallowness of their dedication to His teachings is apparent in the condition of the world; as it is now and as it was in Christ's time. This is the result of a belief – a condition of mind which obscures the reality of the situation – one of Maya's tools of deception.

There are people who believe that Christ was a fool to die as He did. Of course, people have all sorts of strange beliefs about what their guru should or should not do, what he should eat, wear, say, etc. They presume to pass judgement on his behaviour. It can be supposed that the great Tibetan Yogi, Milarepa, would never have repented for his murderous past and would not have evolved if he had had this judgemental sort of attitude towards his guru. Milarepa, or Jetsun as he was then called, was a master of the Black Arts. He was strongly conditioned by his former beliefs and practices, and he had great power to control others. However, he could not within the scope of his knowledge absolve himself from the bad karma he had enacted. For this, he had to surrender to the Master, Marpa, who told him, as penance, to build a house. That task completed, he was instructed to destroy the house and return each stone where he had originally found it. He was then told to rebuild the house . . .

destroy . . . and rebuild again . . .

This could certainly be regarded as peculiar behaviour for a Master by one without understanding. One might wonder what sort of a High Being this is? Similarly, humans often lament, "What kind of God is this who has created so much misery and suffering?" But has He, really? When things go well, everything appears to be beautiful and the human ego is eager to take the credit. But when things go wrong, who gets the blame?

The problem is that humankind does not understand – cannot begin to fathom – the mystery of God's working. Rather than seek the Truth through dedication and hard spiritual work, the human being finds it much easier to attach labels to situations, thoughts and objects in order to categorize, theorise and to 'conclude'. It is hoped that this will bring peace of mind. What really results, though, is catastrophic misconceptions and unreal conditioning. In the societies now existent on earth, millions of females are fighting a battle against male conditioning. Conversely, males are upset that females have been conditioned against them. Eastern civilizations have been conditioned to think that the people of Western countries are all demonic, hedonistic materialists. Westerners do not trust Easterners . . .

Throughout the world people are conditioned to believe they are fighting for what is right. Consider religious wars and the matter of race. The problem is that all this conditioning prevents clear thinking – people are not able to know what is really 'right'. There is collective conditioning that creates a climate in which creatures can be killed, eaten, used for scientific experimentation or other whims of humankind who believes it is superior. The human ego has been deluded by the feeling that it is powerful – "I am the boss, I am no one's servant, I will be served." This is the sound of a distorted condition of mind, enveloping an ailing ego. Nothing but negativity can be bred by such aberration of mind, ego, psyche and soul.

The human ego enjoys asserting itself. Every now and then it gives in to the temptation to illustrate its existence by acting in a manner which is magnified and distorted. It becomes a caricature of itself. Blown out of proportion, literally bloated with pride and self-concern, it will seek, over and over again, opportunities to show its superiority. Just how often this pompous self-aggrandizement occurs is a measure of the ego's sickness. What is really being illustrated is a sense of inferiority, creating the need to put on a disguise. This is an aberrant ego. There is another way in which the ego can be manifest. A healthy ego can expand itself, realizing its god-like qualities. This implies simultaneous realization of humankind's responsibility to evolve to the state of godliness. If this is confusing to you, Maya has her hands over your eyes.

There is much talk these days of 'finding oneself' and 'knowing' one's (little) self. It is useless. However, if one identifies with God, one will act in a god-like manner, manifesting integrity, responsibility and purity rather than the petty prizes of the ego's duality game; competitiveness, avarice, aggression, lust, loneliness and alienation from others, and many more negative products of a distorted condition of mind.

The ego tries to trick God or guru into doing favours for it. It is a manipulator, a deal-maker. In its worst manifestation the ego will even allow the rest of the human being to be destroyed rather than admit it is wrong. Suicide is an example of the ego convincing the human to perish rather than change some condition of mind which would 'kill' the ego. "If I can't have it my way, I quit." "I'll never change . . . accept me as I am or not at all." "This is the way I am – I want to be good, but . . . " These are all symptoms of a distorted and corrupt ego which is attempting to prevent growth. Ego has conditioned the mind to believe it cannot live without ego. With Maya's help it has made itself the most important thing on earth.

In order to grow, a human being must destroy this diseased ego by breaking through its barrier of false conditioning. One must identify with the immortal selfless Self rather than the petty, selfish self. The guru can help here if one actually listens to his teachings without colouring the words with what the ego wishes to hear. The ego is expert at misinterpreting the Truth and twisting it to serve its own ends. One must learn the technique of living correctly. 'Right living' is a skill which lies dormant within each human being and must be uncovered. But Maya'a clutter must first be swept away. All conditions must be broken. When there are no more conditions, one will have come home.

One must not be tied to objects, ideas, beliefs or fantasies; must give up identification with gross forms of ego-projection; must overcome habit, 'good' or 'bad'; must forget the fruits of one's labours – there is no use manipulating God by 'acting' like one who deserves enlightenment. And one must fight against discouragement. What is needed is acceptance of the challenge, constant vigilance and awareness of the Maya at work within ourselves (use the tools of meditation and contemplation). One must have the realization that enlightenment is the human being's birthright – it is promised to him if he seeks in earnest and does not falter when presented with confusion and difficulties (use the tool of mindfulness). When one's lower urges have been transformed, through constant effort and self-discipline, into passion for growth and the longing for enlightenment – through the tools of sadhana and tapasya (spiritual practice and austerity) – God will reveal Itself!

Consider once more the matter of appearances. Listen to these words, "Maya / matter / mater / mother." To treat Maya as an adversary would indeed be negative. She must be appreciated as the matrix in which every human being is being born, nourished and evolved. She is the medium through which enlightenment is attained. She is your mother. When you seek to understand her with the love of a child, she will help you grow. And you will leave her one day when you have outgrown the need of her protective cocoon.

3
The Fruit of Purity

Therefore let your soul exalt your reason to the height of passion
That it may sing and let it direct your passion with reason
That your passion may live through its own daily resurrection
And like a phoenix rise above its own ashes.

KAHLIL GIBRAN

The human being cannot achieve a state of consciousness inharmonious with its nature. No amount of eagerness and resolve can alter this fact. The nature must be changed through enlightened effort, conscientious discipline and subservience to the law of sacrifice. This prepares the being for the coming of the Soul. Purification of mind and body is essential for one who seeks enlightenment. One cannot expect to experience the highest state of consciousness by practising a few hatha yoga poses or repeating mantra. The way to liberation is an arduous path which requires total dedication and faultless preparation. Every aspect of the individual's existence must be devoted to the cause. Any act which does not serve the higher purpose must eventually be sacrificed for one that does. Communion with God is the highest; such powerful energies are not perceived if one is not attuned to the higher wave-length, nor if one's motives are impure.

Consider the words of Shankaracharya, who wrote in the 8th century, "Without knowledge there is no nirvana." To what sort of knowledge did he make reference? A Sanskrit dictionary defines the meaning of nirvana as 'dissolution, death or final emancipation from matter and reunion with the Supreme Spirit . . . annihilation of individual existence or of all desires and passions . . . perfect calm, highest bliss'. Is knowledge that distilled essence of everything thought, seen, heard, read or experienced, which is stored since birth and beyond in the human mind? Or could it be something beyond the perception of mind? The truth is that the unevolved human mind is not a fit receptacle for the pure and total knowledge of which Shankaracharya speaks. Profound knowledge becomes clouded by subjective judgements and desires; it cannot be perceived if the mind is full of false convictions, prejudices and irrational excesses. The impure mind will seek to turn all of life to its own purpose and invariably distorts and tarnishes the illuminating qualities of pure knowledge.

In order to perceive the knowledge which leads to nirvana, one must develop what Patanjali has called 'soul vision'. Thereby one can wear away the hindrances to understanding, the darkness of unwisdom, self-assertion, lust, hate, attachment . . . The eyes must be opened, the veils removed, that the spiritual being may come into power over body and mind. The spirit alone can assimilate the knowledge of bliss which is not worldly. The realization of the divine spirit within can only come from a pure and courageous heart, focused resolutely upon the Eternal. The mind must be purified, subdued and detached from the confusion of joy and grief. Yet knowledge alone is not enough to release one from the web of illusion. Unwisdom is more often born of attachment than of ignorance.

The story of Krishna and Sudama is a fine example of such absence of 'soul vision' and attachment to lower desires.

Two boys, who called themselves friends, Krishna and Sudama, studied under the guidance of the Guru Sandeepni. Sudama was the elder of the two, so Krishna called him 'Bhaya', a respectful term for brother. As they prepared one day to collect firewood in the forest, the wife of their guru gave them a bowl of chickpeas to take along as food supply. Being the oldest boy, Sudama took charge of the chickpeas, and off they went.

In the forest they were caught by a heavy rainstorm and found refuge for the night beneath a large mango tree. In the cold dampness they sat, two friends sharing one blanket, huddled together against the darkness. Assuming the yoga pose of withdrawal, siddhasana, they contemplated the lessons of their guru, finding peace even in that moment of adversity. That is, rather, what Krishna did. Sudama, on the other hand, began to feel a gnawing hunger. Sitting there in the dark, his contemplation turned to chickpeas and the problem of how little he had. "If I gave Krishna half the peas, that would not leave enough for me." So he concluded he should eat all the chickpeas given for him and his smaller friend . . . reasoning, perhaps, that he must remain strong to lead his companion . . . he being the elder. This he did, secretively, taking small mouthfuls and hoping Krishna would not notice. The peas were so hard that they broke with a cracking sound under the greedy tooth pressure of Sudama. Krishna knew what was happening, but asked innocently, "What is that noise, Bhaya?" Sudama replied, "I am shivering, that was the noise of my teeth" . . . half a lie.

Krishna, the divine mind, was playing the human lila. If he had really wished, the goddess of food, Annapurna, would have brought all the delicious morsels of the world to him. Poor Sudama, with his limited perspective, was doing the unforgivable. In India it is considered sinful to eat while a younger person goes hungry; besides, he was negating the bond of friendship. This karmic foible would have devastating effects on Sudama's life in later years.

Despite his education and high qualifications Sudama grew up to be a pauper. So poor he could not even afford one meal a day, he lived in misery and shame, and he could never over-come the guilt that had haunted him since childhood. Krishna had become the Emperor and was renowned as the greatest being on Earth. Sudama's wife tried repeatedly to persuade him to go and beg help of his former friend. But the poor fellow could not muster enough courage to face the friend he had once loved. After much nagging, he gave in to his wife's wishes; her life, after all, was also made miserable by her husband's bad karma. As he set off for Krishna's palace, his wife gave him a little rice, which was all they had. It is a custom that when you visit a friend you take some gift. They tied the rice in an old rag, which Sudama carried under his arm.

The long journey brought him at last to the island abode of

Krishna, a glorious palace of marble and gold in the midst of an ocean. At the entrance, Sudama was stopped by the guards who were greatly amused that a pauper had the audacity to insist he was a friend of the great Krishna. He must be confusing the Emperor with another person of the same name . . . surely, the man was deluded. Sudama insisted he would wait until he saw Krishna, would die there if need be, but would not leave. So he became a subject of many jokes around the palace environs . . . the situation was laughed at from guard to guard, finally permeating the palace itself. At last, the court entertainer related the story to the Emperor through Sanskrit poetry; the meaning roughly: there is a man outside the gate who has no clothes, no shoes, whose feet are bleeding and sore. He has so little flesh one can see his bones. His garment is torn and ragged; he carries a stick in his hand and gestures wildly that he must see his friend Krishna . . . is this not a joke? And his name, he says, is Sudama.

Hearing that name, Krishna jumped up from his throne, dropping his royal chadra (his cloak), and rushed out to the gate. Astonished, his court followed. He took Sudama in his arms, saying, "Why did you never inform me? You should have come long before." He dragged his weary friend into the palace and placed him on the throne. Putting the bruised feet in his lap he began to massage them and wept at the condition of his childhood friend, thereby washing the feet. It is a custom to wash the feet of one's guest, so that the tiredness may go.

Sudama was bewildered to be seated on the throne, and when his great friend accused him of hiding something, he felt deeply ashamed. How could he offer this miserable bundle of rice? But Krishna took it and began to eat. He ate one handful, then another, and as he reached for the last bit, the queen stopped him. For by eating the gift, he was giving; the queen feared he would give everything away and nothing would be left of his vast empire. That was the extent of Krishna's generosity.

For three days Sudama lived in luxury. (Three days is the minimum length of visit in India.) Then he said he had to go and see his wife. As he left, Sudama felt an emptiness. "What was the use in coming?" He thought "It was a good time for three days. But now I go away just as I came. He gave me nothing, though his wealth is great."

Sudama had become a devotee of Krishna, who was obviously a High Being, but he had imperfect faith. Once again his mind was set on negativity. His perspective remained as limited as it had been in the beginning, when he planted the seeds of his own suffering. Nevertheless, he had felt the grace of Krishna and was lifted up for some time, however fleeting. What would he tell his wife? How could he explain that he had brought her nothing? As he approached his land, he could see no village. His mudhouse was gone and a palace stood on the premises. He had to be lost. In the distance he saw women in beautifully coloured saris; they smiled at him. Whatever strange, happy place this was, it wasn't his home. He turned to walk the other way, thinking he had become confused, probably because he was preoccupied with such depressing throughts. The people of his village recognized him and called after him, "Why do you turn away, don't you know us?" They greeted him with reverence and began to do arati – the offering of light. Astonished and humbled, Sudama came to understand that Krishna had given him a palace and kingdom of his own. Gradually he saw that the divine mind forgives, while the limited mind focuses always on the negative side. He had always been a selfish friend, while Krishna had given him two-thirds of his kingdom and would have given more, had the queen not intervened. And he saw that he was the cause of his own suffering.

Sudama represents the soul-personality and Krishna the Godhead. If you behave like a soul-personality, if you identify with human limitations, you will suffer your entire life. However, if your eyes are open, if you are conscious and can identify with your divine aspects, it will be much easier to handle each situation in order to progress.

Sudama has no eye to see who Krishna is, although it is Krishna's kindness to associate with Sudama. There is no need for Krishna to call Sudama his friend. Krishna is complete in himself. Throughout his life Krishna manifests this completeness in every situation and relationship. As a child, he is the complete child; as guru, he is the complete guru; and as friend, he is the complete friend. Friendship for Krishna means a total commitment, an everlasting bond, complete attunement – a continuous flow of being. But Sudama, caught in greed, ego and emotion, is unable to realize this truth. Although he has direct association of the Godhead Himself, he does not recognize who he is with, even when he experiences the most profound manifestation of loving and forgiving friendship . . . as Krishna runs and embraces his old friend, "Why didn't you come before?"

You are surrounded by teachers, but you do not heed their instructions. The words of gurus, the writings of Great Ones, nature, maya, sun, moon . . . all of this earth and its spatial environment can be your university. Unfortunately humans have a tendency to filter everything through their own personalities; the almighty ego becomes interpreter. In the resulting confusion God Him/Herself would not be recognized if encountered face to face. When truth and compassion are offered, the self-concerned human fails to see the value thereof. Ego demands attention and fulfilment of its desires; it needs to be 'appreciated'.

To gain liberation from the tyranny of the ego, you must pay the keenest attention to yourself and your world. Quietly observe and contemplate, without drawing hasty conclusions and erroneous assumptions prompted by those old bits of information kept undusted on the shelves inside your mind.

Concentrate, for instance, on the moon. What can be learned from this ancestor of earth? Besides marking time in measurements of months, she moves the tides and influences the fluids of the human bloodstream, thus affecting the ebb and flow of emotion. The moon appears to be in a constant state of transformation. Imagine the first primitive little being who noticed the 'disappearance' of the moon. Frightened of the darkness, he may have spurned the phantom with "Who needs you anyway? Shine a little while and then you leave me . . . no warning . . . it just left . . . it's an omen!" So much excitement and turmoil for no reason. If our imaginary little Neanderthaler had waited and watched with some poise and detachment, he may have gained insight, instead of wasting his energy.

The darkness of the new moon can herald the beginning of awareness of the Spirit. It can bring the birth of new understanding to one who is attuned. The stars do not die from the glare of the sunshine which obscures them; low tide at the seashore does not indicate that the ocean has evaporated. Similarly, when the moon cannot be seen, it has not gone away. A silver sliver in the sky is not less moon than a full circle of light. It is 'Avidya-maya', spiritual ignorance, illusion, lack of wisdom which makes it seem so. In all her manifestations the moon is as constant as the purity of the Soul which transcends time, space, periodicity and emotional cycles.

A tiny seed, when planted in earth, is unseen to the human eye. It goes through a period of gestation which could be considered the most miraculous time in its development. Like magic the components of its being are energized and fertilized by nutrients and mysterious properties of water and soil. A kind of miniature atomic explosion occurs in that darkness, unseen and silent to human ears. Shoot breaks through shell of seed, becomes plant, reaches to the barrier of the surface and pokes through to grow sufficiently tall to be noticed by the human eye. It 'appears' between the earth's floor and the ceiling of the stars. But it was there all along. It is one of nature's illustrations. Such lessons are everywhere, in infinite variety. But one who already has all the answers will be unable to see beyond the periphery of the ego's shroud. In that case, knowledge is of no use.

The need to be right in every situation – more often a cover for feelings of inadequacy – will obstruct the flow of truth and perpetrate the darkness of unwisdom. Though few can discern right from wrong when confronted with situations in their own lives, many pretend to understand what is being said by Wise Ones. In truth, they are not listening. When questioned on some aspect of their behaviour, they devise all manner of circuitous evasions of truth. It is as if life itself depended on keeping the truth under wraps. This senseless need to be right results in much wrong behaviour. Millions have died in battles caused by a few individuals ego-locked in argument over whose God or which ideology was the (only) right one.

Arrogance, criticism and competition are products of self-absorption which intercept knowledge. Attempting to promote one's superiority by degrading others is blatant violation of the law of ahinsa, the law of non-injury. The temptation to judge is equal folly and should be resisted. After all, by what authority is one human given the right to judge another . . . by the authority of the ego? You should know that every time you think badly of someone, you accept some of that person's negative karma. Negativity attracts negativity; hence the importance of maintaining a positive vibration through cultivation of positive thought and feeling. Strive to do *your* work . . . live *your* life as perfectly as possible, without hindering the progress of others. By putting stumbling blocks in the path of others, you obstruct your own growth. Envy, anger and hatred cannot take you where you want to go, but make your quest a failure. A tremendous amount of energy is spent in negative distractions – energy which should be channelled elsewhere.

Shakespeare mentioned that the cackling of geese would drown the song of the nightingale. The beautiful energy of God is hampered by the negative charge of arrogance. Like a bad connection on the telephone line, the truth in words spoken by the guru will not be received by minds fettered with biases, previous programming or egotistical imaginings. The effect of past karma and samskara can be devastating, if not modified by present good works and diligent spiritual practice. A shield of negativity, created and strengthened by repetition, can grow into hardened armour. Its only effectiveness is in protecting you from the truth. The shield of misconception must be worn thin enough to allow the freshening breeze of pure truth and profound knowledge to touch the fledgeling spirit beneath. For, as Mahatma Gandhi said, "The instruments for the quest of truth are as simple as they are difficult.

They may appear quite impossible to the arrogant person, yet most natural to an innocent child. The seeker after truth should be humbler than the dust. The world crushes the dust under its feet, but the seeker after truth should so humble himself that even the dust could crush him. Only then, and not until then, will he have a glimpse of truth."

Assumptions are miscarriages of truth that often go unnoticed, until caught in mid-air by the eagle-like insight of a Wise One. Faulty interpretation translates what was true into what is false. It may seem convenient to 'adjust' the meaning of lessons and disciplines to suit one's own purposes, but such manipulation backfires on the perpetrator. "The ideal of truth requires that vows taken should be fulfilled in the spirit as well as in the letter," but " . . . selfishness turns them blind, and by the ambiguous middle they deceive themselves and seek to deceive the world and God". Gandhi's words are clear enough. Whether caused by laziness, lack of courage or hypocrisy, stretching the truth by assuming is both dangerous and wasteful. "Guruji, I assumed I could do that . . . I thought you meant that . . . " Failure to grow results from such miscalculations.

Seekers after comfort and romance will be sadly disappointed on the spiritual path. If your goals in life are set on the manifestations of maya, you will not find your source of fulfilment, which is not without, but *within*. Like a mouse on a treadmill, you may get lots of exercise and some experience; but the endless repetition cannot lead you out of the maze of illusion in which you are imprisoned. Exasperation, frustration, desperation and despair are the souvenirs of that journey. Your grief will extend to those around you, who will be affected by your cloud of negativity – and who will be blamed for your distress. Many marriages have ended because people who were never happy while single, marry and put the blame of their unhappiness upon their spouses.

Humans continuously project their own desires, beliefs and opinions on the world around them. Spiritual teachings, myths and histories of Gods and Great Ones are often sensualized, so that the true meaning is obscured by subjectivity and romantic illusion. The beauty of the truth, if one could but see it, would far surpass the fabrication of superficial interpretation. The limited mind reflects itself upon everything it encounters, including the teachings of High Beings. The assumed sensuality, for instance, of Lord Krishna's play with the many gopis – the milkmaids of Brindaban – who cared for him as a baby, has been a prolific source of rapturous celebration in paintings and prose. The theme, usually portrayed with ample eroticism, might be put into clearer perspective with the realization that Baby Krishna was indeed adored, but the frolicking ended when he left them at age eleven! Close scrutiny of Sanskrit texts also reveals that Radha, often referred to as his lover and chosen one, was married and had borne children before meeting with the adult Krishna. At that time she was herself an enlightened being, far beyond the temptations of romance. They met and spent a few hours together in spiritual discussion, rather than sensual communion. Thousands of years have kept this story's true essence buried beneath the romantic imaginings of the unenlightened mentality.

Picture the God Shiva (Śiva) and his consort Parvati.* Contemplation will reveal the symbolic lessons of their existence together. In Sanskrit 'Parvati' can signify: fullness and also rock, stone, rugged as of a mountain. Parvati is the feminine aspect, the Shakti energy of Shiva. The same feminine form of the name, Śivā, represents final emancipation. Shiva, often referred to as the Great God and the Dispeller of Illusions, is said to have one thousand and eight names. As the third god of the Aryan triad – after Brahma, the Creator and Vishnu, the Preserver – he is the Destroyer, the Three-Eyed One who annihilates all negativity. He not only put Kama (desire) to ashes with a glance of his third eye; the same fate befell both Brahma and Vishnu and implies his sovereignty. Shiva is in charge not only of destruction but also has dominion over

---

* Correct accentuation is indispensible to the precise meaning of Sanskrit terms. The intention here is not to present concise accentuation but is for the point of differentiation. The given examples show the effect of accentuation upon the meaning of the word.

regeneration and rebirth. He is the Auspicious One. The moon's crescent over his central eye marks the division of time into months; the serpent at his neck measures years and the skulls and other serpents about his body represent the perpetual revolution of ages and successive extinction and generation of the races of humanity.

The combining of the powerful male principle of Vidya (truth), revealed by the Dispeller of Illusion, with the female principles of endurance (rock) and fullness (completeness) produced a child: Ganesh, who is a symbol of wisdom. As theorized by the psychologist Carl Gustav Jung, all beings have within them male and female aspects which, when brought into union with each other, will create harmony within the psyche. Disunion results in discord and disruption of the being's balance. Attempts to achieve self-fulfilment, through uniting with others outside of Self, is a distortion of this principle and fails to achieve the goal. Taking the theory further, within the context of spiritual life, one can see that Shiva and Śivā are one and the same, as symbolized by the Sivarudra image which is half male and half female. One is correct in saying that union of the two aspects of Self on the spiritual plane will lead to completeness. View Shiva/Parvati as energies rather than individuals.

Growth is not always a pleasurable experience and can involve tremendous hardship and pain, both physical and mental. Parvati's extreme asceticism in the mountains and the fires of penance she endured in order to burn away her imperfections and illusions attest to the fact. Though the fates had decreed her position as Shiva's consort through many lifetimes, she had to earn her own emancipation under the command and guidance of her guru. As Shiva's chief disciple, her mistakes had disastrous consequences: in an earlier incarnation she was Uma – Shiva's helper, friend, and lover. (Derived from the Sanskrit Ud-ma, this could also mean 'gem lying on the surface', and called, hailed, commanded.) Shiva's disappointment at Uma's mistake – she had doubted Him – caused Shiva to withdraw. She, who had been the shining gem of all disciples, made a fatal error in not realizing the profound truth of Shiva's relationship to Lord Rama. The withdrawal of Shiva was no ordinary thing. To atone for her mistake, Uma had to leave her body and await rebirth as Parvati, who was enduring and rugged, with the stability of mountains and the wisdom never again to question. She followed the Siva-marga through fervent asceticism in her mountain abode under the watch of Shiva. She mastered the various Yogas and attained realization, Sivamukti.

When one subjects oneself to discipline as a disciple, one seeks to become the result of that discipline. In Parvati's case, she became Śivā. They were always the same. She had to purify herself to remove the illusion of duality. If one is disciple of Christ, Buddha, Mohammed, etc., one follows His teachings in order to become the Being and to live in the Light. The personification or personality is not important. The goal is to become the ideal which is taught. Becoming the knowledge is what leads to nirvana. That is the meaning of some High Beings becoming missions in themselves.

Without purification, there can be no illumination. There is a speck of divinity within each human being waiting to be nurtured and strengthened. An army of spiritual aides await the command; you have only to issue the order and your campaign is begun. Take up the challenge to defeat your misconception of yourself, your world and your God. In this battle against ignorance you will be armed with the powerful weapons of ahinsa, aparigraha, meditation, contemplation, spiritual reading, and obedience to guru. Your efforts will wear down the hindrances, remove barriers and allow the embryonic godliness to expand and grow. Remember that the enemy is not outside, trying to get in; you are the enemy. Every time you take an action, say a word or produce a thought which is counter to growth, you stand in the way of your own pursuit of liberation. You need to free yourself from the stranglehold of your ego which runs you like a robot. With the same sense of power you feel pressing remote control buttons to switch channels on the television, the ego pushes *your* buttons: you experience anger, jealousy, grief and the occasional warmth of some victory often obtained at the expense of another whom you have 'beaten' at one of Maya's foolish games. You will have to overcome the programming and gain control of yourself! Defeat the fanatical ego and release the prisoner within. Unlike other wars against tyranny, this one produces no casualities. The sick ego is merely restored to health and proper perspective.

The mind must be brought under the control of the Spiritual Being. Thought must be controlled by will. You will have to develop a network of superintelligence in order to spy on yourself; constant vigilance will win you the freedom you crave. It is not easy. You may only go part of the way this lifetime. The supreme goal of existence cannot be achieved without supreme effort. When you have developed the genius of the Soul, you will comprehend the knowledge leading to nirvāna . . . and that is the fruit of purity.

4

I am in the Expanse of the Heart

Only when the flesh is passive, head cool,
Soul as pure and firm as fiery diamond
Will the radiance reach the chamber,
Its sunlight warm the heart.

SVĀMI PŪRṆĀ

One sunny day during a jet flight over mountainous terrain, an inquisitive passenger contemplated the beauty below and was shocked to notice sudden, lightning-like flashes cross valleys and hills. Atop one mountain roamed a shimmering rivulet, gone instantly, replaced further on by a larger stream of light – shining, sparkling, twisting rapidly in serpentine patterns over the earthscape. Was it illusion? Dots of light appeared and vanished like twinkling, fading stars or messages from another realm. The observer became entranced by these ephemeral flames and flickers of light. In a dance of birth and death more exquisite than any form of man-made artifice, swift-spreading webs of fire delighted the seeker's attention, seeming to whisper, "Remember . . . me . . . remember who I am." Remember what? Whatever the meaning of this message from nature, it could not be understood through eyes and ears alone.

Without sunlight reflected upon them, the waters below did not exist to the observer, appearing only as he was moved to an angle where the sun's reflection could be seen. Although the rivers were always there and light was also constant in the short time that passed, beginning and ending were reflections in the eye of the beholder. Yet, some speck of truth, illustrated below in mysterious code, touched the heart of the seeker.

Thousands of years ago King Janaka the 'Videha' (one who

holds the body but is beyond body) asked, "What is the soul?" He was answered by the great sage Yajnavalkya, "It is the consciousness of life . . . the light of the heart." In the *Bhagavad Gita*, Krishna calls the soul " . . . prince victorious which dwells in the heart of all things . . . beginning . . . middle . . . end of all that lives."

Ancient Vedic texts like *Mu–daka Upanishad* state, "He who knows Him dwelling in the secret place of the heart cuts asunder the bonds of ignorance even in the human life . . . radiant in his light, yet invisible in the secret place of the heart."

Chandogya Upanishad elaborates further, "There is a light that shines beyond all things on earth, beyond us all, beyond the heavens, beyond the highest, the very highest heavens. This is the Light that shines in our hearts . . . in the centre of the castle of Brahman, our own body, there is a small shrine in the form of a lotus flower . . . within can be found a small space . . . the little space within the heart is as great as this vast universe."

Maitri spoke, "He who is in the sun and in the fire and in the heart of man is One. He who knows this is one with the One."

Visualize the sun. Regard it as one of billions with a greater sun at the source. Considering the magnanimity exuded by such being puts meagre dramas of separate egos into perspective. Each human being, microcosm of this gigantic energy system, has a solar plexus for the reception of cosmic energy – blessings of the Source. We are individual rays of the Source, and it shines freely through us when not limited by the barriers we impose upon ourselves. As mind and body purify, lighten and become more subtle, the being becomes filled with energy, readily received and held. Physical form is merely a net – Source manifests unfettered. With ego's tyranny removed, the unchained heart becomes a vast, glorious chalice to be filled with Divine Light. Contemplate upon this Light which fills the heart; remember always that one must be empty to be filled, open to receive.

The solar plexus is a network of nerves and blood vessels lying between ribs and lower abdomen and covering an area approximately the size of one hand. Energy – cosmic, 'psychic' and otherwise – is said to enter the body at this point. Most humans allow energy to be depleted in frivolous mental/ physical activity, negative thinking and aimless conversation. However, when psychic energy is held, preserved and directed properly, it can be used in Source-striving activities . . . those at the heart, gem of the solar plexus. Economical and systematic use of energy is a secret of the Yogis.

Prana has a mysterious effect upon the heart, as do emotions. Pranayama expands the solar plexus and nourishes the heart. Notice how shallowness of breath accompanies negative emotions, and compare to the blissful infusion of energy resulting from peaceful, equalized breathing. Such figures of speech as 'strong-hearted, heartless, cold-hearted, heart of gold, hearty, heartfelt, heartache, take to heart, memorize by heart, etc. . . . ', describe more than a fleshy, bloodpumping organ. Is it mere symbolism which has placed the heart so reverently at the centre of thinking and feeling since antiquity? An English dictionary defines it as the 'core, central, vital, main part, innermost thought centre of emotions and personality attributes'. There must be valid reasons why the heart is universally held in higher esteem than the rest of the human form.

The universal heart is full of courage, love, compassion, truth and light. Yogis consider its human counterpart a receptacle of bliss, an organ of enlightenment. It is believed that the Kundalini Shakti – the divine creative energy – when activated, rises by way of a nadi (nerve) which leads in a serpentine manner to the crown chakra, centre of highest spiritual dominion. The top of the head may be felt to disappear, as barriers between human and God disintegrate and the mind is opened to the heavens. Consciousness then directs energy downwards to its final destination, the heart, where karma and those old mental impressions, accumulated over many lives, are devoured in flames in realization. Few are attracted to the tremendous effort, self-control and devotion essential to evolution. None, however, can totally ignore the beckoning of the Cosmic Heart, answered with longing within one's own core. It must one day be fulfilled. That unity is the goal of existence, the ending of the great illusion, which sees the One as two.

A young student of metaphysics once wrote:

. . . and blest are those
Whose blood and judgement are so well commingled
That they are not a pipe for fortune's finger
To sound what stop she pleases. Give me that man
That is not passion's slave, and I will wear him
In my heart's core, ay, in my heart of heart,
As I do thee.

Thus spoke Hamlet, through the pen of Shakespeare.

The human mind uses symbols to 'see', to reach conclusions, to understand in a finite mode. It relates and compares opposites. Herein lies the creation of duality, the delusion of fragmentation. Mind is unable to perceive the Infinite while focused on every detail of duality. At some levels of consciousness religious symbols are helpful; ritual is effective only when resulting in growth. Ancient Buddhist wisdom states that 'once the animal is caught, the snare can be discarded'. Once ideas conveyed by words are understood, the words are no longer needed. Ritual falls away naturally when all actions are consecrated.

The Source within radiates energy in all directions, like the spokes of a Wheel. One may progress through many layers of consciousness before merging entirely into the Source. At times one finds others at a similar stage in relationship to the goal. The temptation to compare growth, to identify so closely with others that the way is forgotten, must be avoided. Individuals may influence each other negatively. One should neither be concerned with the growth of others, nor with one's own. The gaze should constantly be fixed upon the Infinite, for all else is duality. Source is the centre. Devotion to God or guru, discipline and dedication of all action bring one nearer to Truth. It is natural to gravitate toward the centre. Magnetism is intensified the closer one comes, until enlightenment brings total unification with the cosmic sun – one's true nature. Negativity, such as doubt or self-concern, instantly cuts the magnetic cord and the individual falls out of orbit, occasionally influencing others to join in leaving the path. Jealousy (acting and reacting with others) magnifies duality, creating tangents which waste energy and mislead. Fervent striving eventually creates absorption into the Source.

The Source is the great heart which corresponds to each individual's core. Modern astrology has discovered that our own galaxy (and others also) is moving swiftly through space, drawn toward some gigantic force. This discovery may be frightening unless one realizes that fear is just another form of duality. Each tiny human creature is born within the same matrix, is one small satellite of the One. Birth and death are just symbols for changes of consciousness. The One always was, is and will be, something only the heart can comprehend. Science has theorized the world's creation as a big bang, a huge explosion of energy. It is not illogical to suppose that a magnificent implosion will reabsorb the worlds. Giving and taking back, expanding and contracting, creation and dissolution are activities of the One. In a similar manner one breathes, inhaling and exhaling in continuous rhythm. Every breath is said to be an unconscious repetition of the name of God. According to mythology, this world and all others are subject to the effect of Shiva's mystical dance of creation and destruction. Science would do well to heed the Vedas. Worlds come and go, Source remains.

One can visualize the Source within one's own heart. But this is a reflection, as if seen in a mirror – it is said to be on the right side. The Bible states, "The wise man's heart is at the right hand side, and the fool's heart is on the left." It is not coincidental that many people place a hand over the right side of the chest in times of shock. It is the centre from which one hundred and one nadis emanate.* From the inner sun paths of energy, nerves, brain impulses and subtle inner galaxies emerge, flow and orbit. It is the energy source . . . the power house. Creative intelligence rests there as well as vasanas – the

* Sushuma nadi curves from the solar plexus through the spinal cord to the brain in Sahasrara nadi, continuing down to the heart via Jivanadi. From this one can understand the application of the Kundalini Serpent symbol.

latent tendencies and blossoms of the karma of separateness. It is a matter of choice which shall be awakened. It is good to remind oneself that just as a mind lost in body consciousness pulls its focus from the heart into an empty shell, comparison with the progress of others does not progress one's own spiritual development. Beware of that which lessens harmony.

One can meditate upon the inner sun and direct prana (life force) into the solar plexus by placing the fingertips of both hands upon the area and concentrating on receiving cosmic energy with inhalation and distribution through the fingertips and exhalation. As always, total relaxation is essential. One can also practice radiating the light of the heart beyond the perimeter of the body. In time of stress, it may be helpful to touch the centre of the chest and place consciousness there; fear will instantly leave. A fiery core, full of activated energy, feels no separation from the protection of the Cosmic Heart.

Spiritual life is not just a conglomerate of fantasy, mythology and allegorical romanticism, though these are the tools of Savitri, inspiration. Cosmic law is inalienable and impervious to human desire and manipulation. Appropriate application of the law constitutes the highest science – metaphysics, science of the heart. That is absolute justice, far removed from any human interpretation of the term. From this view, consider the properties of the 'castle of Brahman', wherein lies the much revered 'heart of heart'. To overcome body consciousness does not imply that the physical shell should be discarded prematurely. The body is a vehicle for the transmutation of the total being. Concentration upon that which transcends the physical realm causes rebirth on the cellular level. The religious expression 'born again' goes deeper than its symbolic meaning. It is said that nine months of hatha yoga, conscientiously executed – with focused consciousness – results in physical rejuvenation. When one transcends gross levels of consciousness, the cells of organs, glands, etc. evolve. In fact, every part of the body is transmuted to a more subtle form.

Emotions are said to issue from glands, rather than from the brain, although there is interaction between all members of the system. "As above, so below." Repetition of sacred mantra affects endocrine activity, as does hatha yoga. Hormones secreted by thyroid adrenals and pituitary can urge one to feel anger, fear, hatred . . . or can provide the impetus to learn and evolve. Adrenals can be depleted of valuable essence by shock, pain, stress and negative thought or emotion, resulting in a lowered resistance to disease, as well as a lesser state of consciousness. Through self-discipline, thought control and dedication to high ideals one can transmute the sex glands which, when reflecting higher levels of consciousness, affect inspirational urges – altruism rather than lust. The gonads are responsible for regeneration and creative power upon the subtle plane. Lasciviousness, greed, jealousy, envy, vengefulness, hostility, etc. can act as potent poisons. The endocrines must work overtime in order to neutralize them chemically. Conversely, meditation, pranayama, spiritual striving, inspirational reading, selfless joy and humanitarian aspirations instigate positive reaction in these 'physical' alchemists, who are then ready to aid evolution. Adrenal hormones are in charge of physical and mental harmony and distribution of energy throughout the organism. When one gland or organ is out of balance or stressed, all are affected. To make up the imbalance or depletion in one, others must exhaust themselves. There is a lesson here beyond physiology.

Each person born into earthly society carries genetic memory of human evolution. For instance, the cells of the bloodstream carry the remnants of a watery past, elements which contain a blood-salt balance as the water-salt balance of the oceans. Pituitary is responsible for that, while thyroid hormones maintain the iodine balance of blood. Each cell possesses memory. All human impulse, karma, subjective thought and collective human mind are imprinted upon these dynamic microchips. As if that were not programming enough, human thought is moulded from the moment of birth by culture, fashion, social mores and desire to conform and be accepted. Perceptions which might be labelled strange, unusual or 'out of this world' are suppressed. Thus we truly become products of those who produced us, sharing common consciousness based upon tradition. Impulses of the heart are stifled by conditioning. Of course, some beings arrive on the earthly plane seeing far beyond it and do not adopt the limitations others wish to apply.

Every aspect of the physical body has a subtle form which corresponds to its gross material manifestation. Senses, organs, nerves, bloodstreams, etc. can be used to seek the Source. Each cell is a microcosm of the whole being, which is a small replica of the ultimate macrocosm. Thought and will impulses reflect upon an intricate inner screen; one can actually be permeated with joy and bliss which extends into every cell, or one can be filled, even physically, with depression and 'psychic' exhaustion. Health of individual organs, the harmony of their interaction, can affect higher growth to some extent. Unfortunately, disease is often manifest. It is a common misconception that disease is merely physical; subtle or psychic disturbances do reflect upon the gross body. Similarly, it is not possible to be truly healthy unless enlightened, despite appearances to the contrary. Many diseases lie dormant for years before they blossom. This corresponds to the latent tendencies of the mind.

There are various approaches to health which bring one closer to the Source. Yoga implies union with the Ultimate and harmony between its many aspects. Bhakti yoga – the path of devotion – may dispel the 'I' and 'my' thought, which binds the soul to the lower self, like a lovely bird caught in a snare. Such inclinations obstruct the current of energy magnetized by humility. Jnana yoga – the path of knowledge – may encourage reception of higher knowledge, transforming mental faculties, which bow in homage to Truth. It is possible through hatha and kriya yogas to effect a gradual cleansing and purifying of the physical shell, all bodily components becoming more subtle implements for divine use. Development of physical and mental faculties through discipline can result in transmutation, in the creation of a more permeable membrane of finer sensitivity to waves of high vibration. Selfless service purifies karma. "One is bound by action," spoke Krishna, "unless action is consecrated. Whatever you do, eat, give or offer, let it be an offering to ME. Whatever you suffer, suffer it for ME. Then you shall be free from the bonds of karma which yield fruits of evil and good. With your soul one in renunciation you shall be free and come unto ME." Giving up selfish works is renunciation; giving up the reward of all work is surrender. Attachment causes stress . . . stress causes disease . . . spiritual surrender ends stress.

Spirituality is not a thing apart from life. It does not consist merely of mantras, yantras and exotic clothing, nor is the soul an entity found lurking and loitering around mountaintops and forests. Minds set upon the trappings and accessories of religious rites do not find fulfilment. Fanaticism and obsession are aberrations of emotion; they imprison the heart and stifle the spirit. Seeking itself is expressive of Source, but one must not become so consumed by the means that the end is forgotten. One is deluded by thoughts of being the 'doer' of actions, by identification with any role dictated by the karmic drama. Let the Source work through you. Do not allow ego to get involved. When one thinks, "I am a disciple . . . I am a householder . . . I am this or that . . . ," one identifies with 'labels'. If one sweeps the floor, is one suddenly a floor-sweeper? Identify only with the Ultimate and do not become deluded by the trickery of one's own ego.

The term sanyasa means renunciation of attachments. One must take sanyasa from doubt, which is the favourite cloak of the unenlightened ego. Intellectualization cannot substitute for trust and open-mindedness. Doubts must be surrendered to the Source, for they serve no constructive purpose, but to confuse thinking and confound the path. What is there to fear? Only loss of ego. One who was disillusioned in the past is not doomed forever to maintain the same pose, as if turned to stone. The very word implies removal of a previously held illusion. Everything outside of Source is illusion. Unless one is already enlightened and perceives the truth as 'one-on-one', one must find an interpreter, liaison, representative of Truth (guru) and put one's confidence there. Devotion may assuage doubt. Service dedicated to God or guru can help subjugate egocentric tendencies. However, the best acts performed without real devotion and selflessness are no better than neglectful acts born of confusion. The grace of God is drawn magnetically into the vacuum created by trust, faith and egoless action. Undeveloped intelligence, lacking discrimination, cannot encompass the scope of reality, but sees its own reflection. One cannot live in the past, yet neurotic mentality is capable of many wonders. In order to uphold the 'rightness' of previous conclusions, the ego can project a continuum of imperfect patterns upon its screen, interpreting life to fit its theme. Its colours come through a crystal prism which is distorted, clouded and soiled by misconceptions. The spectrum is marred. Though one's doubts may be dear, and so familiar, they must be surrendered. Profound truth is often paradoxical, not following the so-called laws of mental perception, which is limited by its very dependence upon duality. The nature of mental comparison is inadequate in the face of that which is measureless. Endless efforts to support doubt with rationality are merely a waste of energy. One cannot learn in any field from a teacher whose knowledge one does not trust. How can one expect blessings to come from that which one disavows? Doubting actually blocks perception. By fighting one pushes away that which one longs to understand. Such tension forms armour unsuited to this battle.

When a strong current of positive energy is projected, negativity sent toward it automatically reflects to the perpetrator with intensified force. One does great harm to oneself by doubting that which is beyond question. Love and doubt do not coexist. The true warrior maintains faith and stability in the face of all contradiction and against all odds. When the Source is finally reached and the heart opened, its pure light eradicates all darkness. 'Blind faith' may see truth more clearly than the doubtful, unstable mind.

Humankind, with its many organs of perception, is well equipped for evolution. Faintness of heart dissuades from accepting the challenge. Fiery stamina, patience and perseverance are well within the bounds of human possibility. There are no spiritual olympics, but it is hoped that the incredible attainments of the body, verging on the miraculous at the limits of ordinary consciousness, might correspond to achievement upon more subtle planes. So much courage, devotion and energy have been focused upon physical endeavours in sports and entertainment; how much more should one expect to devote toward spiritual responsibilities?

Thoughts have weight, substance and subtle form. They do not disperse, but remain suspended in the subtle sphere, awaiting further impetus to manifest in grosser form on the material plane. Thoughts travel; they are impulses of will beamed into space, carriers of energy. Groups of people thinking similarly may manifest materially. Thoughts can be focused powerfully through mental discipline acquired in meditation, which is supported by pranayama and physical exercises. Some yogis, strong at heart, have more concentrated and accumulated energy than hundreds of millions of ordinary minds combined. Self-denial (destruction of ego) increases will-power.

It is said that one who is at one with the One can create and destroy worlds at will. It is indeed fortunate that power of such magnitude is never entrusted to those unliberated from the yearnings of ego and latent tendencies. Those who crave miraculous powers would do well to contemplate the source of their desires, in order to prevent insatiable appetites from developing obsessions.

Svetasvatara Upanishad quotes, "The chariot of the mind is drawn by wild horses which have to be tamed . . . With upright body, head and neck, lead the mind and its powers into the Heart, and the Om of the Brahman will be thy boat with which to cross rivers of fear."

Atmospheres created by human thought may endure for hundreds of centuries. Notice the reverence and solemnity evoked upon entering ruins of ancient temples. One may feel repulsion within the environs of ancient sacrificial ritual. This feeling is not mere fantasy. Whenever strong emotion is felt, a substantial manifestation of energy occurs in the subtle realm. This is a secret of the world's best theatrical performers, who must use energy to fill vast stages.

It is said the one thing arrows cannot pierce is thought. Here lies the basis of 'magic' and psychic warfare, as well as healing. Caution regarding thought is important. Thinking is an activity bearing great responsibility, a cause precipitating an effect, however subtle in revelation. This is the source of much self-torture and disease. Words, thoughts, glances of the eye are carriers of energy. At times, numbers of people seem to think 'along the same lines' at the same time in different parts of the world, as if something were 'in the air'. Something is. It can imbue entire populations with vagueness, oppressive feelings or a distorted sense of nationalism. The purified energy created by one realized soul affects the atmosphere positively. One High Being cannot, however, be expected to absorb all the negative karma created by others. It is better to think positively than negatively, but the highest beings do not think at all. Contemplate your own responsibility for thought . . . and the term 'open minded'.

When the inner sun is activated and Source realized within, mind becomes servant of higher perception. Limitless creative intelligence flows from the heart in unending streams of blissful enlightenment. One can execute mundane duties without resorting to thought. Moments of creative genius never involve thinking. Energy is wasted in perpetual motion of circuitous reasoning. When action is performed freely, passionlessly, neither grief nor joy is felt; there is no sense of 'doership', and bliss cancels out lower feelings and impulses.

Many interesting things are encountered upon the super-scientific path. The third eye, for instance, is an entity which allows a spiritually evolved being to see with the corporeal eyes closed. It is related to the pineal gland, situated inward of the area slightly above and between the eyes. Stimulation of this gland is said to cause psychic phenomena; clairvoyance, telepathy, clairaudience and astral travel, as well as mediumship. Shiva's laser-like use of third eye power to incinerate demons and gods alike was not merely symbolic but rather an ability undeveloped by ordinary beings. Examination of the pineal gland shows remarkable similarity in cell structure to the retina of the other two organs of sight. Called the 'light within that reflects the light without', it is a link between higher consciousness and material expression. The source of the third eye lies embedded in the brain, not pasted decoratively on the face. One can meditate upon this area and direct prana, life force, there for achievement of subtle vision.

All life is goal oriented. Observe the growth of vegetation. Watch sunflowers turn their faces to the sun. Notice the persistent travail of ant civilization or the delicate intricacies of one spider's unique web – profound determination and individually creative ability reflect through its pattern. The higher the consciousness, the greater the goal. Few humans dare take upon themselves the relative burden of an ant. Unfortunately, enlightenment is not in fashion, is not the norm so avidly imitated. Purity is widely misconceived; the natural state is thought to be impure, as if one must be changed to something alien in order to be pure. Thus, negativity is accentuated and accepted without much notice. Actually, purity is the most natural state. It is being within the Source, essence of purity. It is abnormal not to be realized; the yogi and the yogini are the normal ones. Indeed, the average man and woman, in a profound sense, manifest pathology. One must have strength of heart to stand outside accepted myths and widely propagated fallacies which obscure the goal. To be full of light, to live in samadhi, is both the goal and one's nature.

There lived in ancient India a powerful king whose wife bore him a son, named Dhruva. The king's attention shifted to another woman, so he discarded the first wife and son to marry the second, who also bore him a son. Dhruva loved to sit upon his father's knee, but the second wife objected, saying hers was the only princely heir who could have that privilege. Confused and dejected, Dhruva pleaded with his mother, who told him it was true – he must forget his wish to sit upon the maharaja's throne. She could see, though, that her son would not be satisfied with any explanation she could give, so she suggested he take his problem to Lord Vishnu, thinking the request would be forgotten with the fervour of prayer. The five year old Dhruva possessed exceedingly strong determination and ventured, with unyielding faith, into the forests surrounding the kingdom. After years of asceticism he came to the 'dwelling' of Lord Vishnu and was met with praise by Narada, the God's servant, who tried to convince the child to turn back. But Dhruva was adamant. He had set out to meet the Lord; there could be no turning back. That was his test. Narada initiated Dhruva, becoming his guru. When eventually reaching the abode of Lord Vishnu, Dhruva wanted to offer praise but knew not what to say. Seeing this, Vishnu pressed his conch to the mouth of the speechless devotee, instantly granting him the gift of understanding. This done, the seeker lost all desire for meaningless power. Wisdom illumined the unreality of the world and he was enlightened. However, he was told to return to the palace and take his place upon the throne; his wisdom would reflect in benevolent rule over the vast kingdom. He was bound to fulfil the karma created by earlier intention. Anything conceived before or during sadhana one must go through. That is why wise beings do not wish anything but maintain a state of void, nothingness. Accordingly, Dhruva had to become not only king, but Emperor of India. After leaving his body, he became 'Lord of the Planets' – embodied in the Morning Star of the Milky Way – a symbol of firm, fixed purpose and perseverance. Such is the power of will.

Stability is a primary requirement for evolution beyond the limits of duality. As if the wild horses of the mind were not difficult enough to control, Maya has devised other distracting influences; extremely subtle qualities of nature called gunas, which affect humans physically, mentally and psychically. These waves of vibration ebb and flow in cycles through all forms of nature in three designations: Sattva, Rajas, Tamas. Sattva is the pure quality, full of light; its brightness manifests bliss, harmony and pure consciousness. Rajas could be called ego; rajasic qualities are stimulating, active, chaotic and hot (spicy food creates a rajasic reaction).

The following list serves as an illustration to increase understanding of the gunas.

I am in the Expanse of the Heart

SATTVA	RAJAS	TAMAS
stability	movement	inertia
bliss	boredom, anxiety	depression
truth-seeking	busy activity	negligence
wisdom	greed	ignorance
heights	middle (crooked path)	lower depths
inspiration	lust/aggression	delusion/doubt
pure thought	mental unrest agitation	irrationality
harmony	chaos	war
vital	frivolous	deadly
light	vagueness	darkness
'I AM' Source	subjective ego duality	gross matter encumbrance
sacrifice with devotion (self-control)	sacrifice for reward (indulgence)	sacrifice without faith (self-torture)
food; pure, fresh health-giving soothing	salty, acidic, sharp, hot, dry, spicy, stimulating	impure, rotten, stale, leftover, preservatives
gifts given from the heart (with faith)	gifts given expecting reward (with manipulation)	gifts given in show (without faith)
consecrated work (renunciation of acts)	work for gain (doership)	work for competition, revenge (morbid)
silence, words of beauty inspiring conversation	frivolous talk gossip/criticism words to influence excite or manipulate others	foul speech verbal attack pornography
light, energy, formlessness	subject (perception with self-concern) ego	object (thinking of people, plants and animals as objects)

Tamas is the signature of darkness, density, decay, corruption and disease. If anger is rajisic, death is tamasic. Stale food, left overnight or devitalized with preservatives and chemical additives, is tamasic, it cannot be expected to produce satvic vitality or harmonious mental states.

Some individuals have more satvic qualities, others are more rajasic or tamasic in nature; most are of mixed temperament. All are subject to the volatile effects of these subtle influences, since human emotion is very changeable. A mind at the mercy of the gunas is as self-determined as a leaf in the wind and may manifest as little integrity. One can transcend the gunas through discipline. To be dominated by rajas binds the soul in attachment to passion, actions and sensationalism. Tamas causes doubt, confusion and negative thought. Even sattva is binding, for its ethereal cloud of matter limits perception of the Infinite. Source is beyond form; all exists within it. When one truly feels 'I am', one is beyond the influence of the gunas.

Krishna said, "When the man or woman of vision sees that the powers of nature are only actors of this vast drama and beholds that which is beyond the powers of nature . . . he comes into my Being . . . and he who with neverfailing love adores me and works for me . . . passes beyond the three powers and can be one with the One."

Absence of duality, unification of Heart, dispassion, detachment and stability dispel the influence of the gunas. A satvic diet is extremely helpful. Just as those who smoke do not always develop lung cancer, it might be argued that attention to physical purity is not essential to spiritual unfolding. The way of yoga is adverse to all aspects of duality – body, mind and soul are parts of the One, interacting harmoniously to serve the highest purpose. Lack of harmony results in pathological symptoms – whether physical, mental or subtle in manifestation. One who seeks liberation has respect for all aspects of Brahman and does not reject any facet of the path. One who is not enlightened, has imperfect judgement. Imagine the folly resulting from self-prescription. Without complete knowledge, how can one say which sadhana is

befitting? Such choice would invariably reflect subjective preference, not the best guide. Accepting responsibility as custodian of the 'castle of Brahman', a seeker takes only the purest
foods – fresh and raw, if possible – and wisely avoids substances such as tobacco, drugs, coffee, tea, alcohol and other
chemicals which distort the entire nervous system.

Death is tamasic. Consumption of animal corpses, whether
fish, fowl, eggs or meat, does not provide satvic vibration.
Karma inherent in the act of killing, whether performed personally or by proxy, encumbers the heart and weakens the
spirit. Karma is also shared; to eat a satvic diet at a table where
meat, fish, etc. is being served is to share in a tamasic activity.
There has been widespread propaganda regarding animal
flesh as a source of protein. Yet vegetable sources actually provide higher quality protein, superior because energy is more
easily assimilated and does not load the body's systems with
toxic waste. The vibration of dairy products may soothe the
nerves and psychic disturbances; best are live cultures of
yoghurt, buttermilk, kefir, etc. which are higher in protein
and well tolerated by most.

It must not be left to imperfect human judgement to determine which fellow earthlings should become human prey.
Fish swimming in the seas and birds traversing the skies are
no less children of Brahman than humans. Many westerners
laugh at, and easterners attempt to rationalize, the reverence
for the sacred cow in India. Since earliest history, this bovine
representative of Mother Earth has gifted humans with abundant milk, a precious substance.

The Vedas spoke of a time when cows were continuously
with milk and plants produced constant harvests, without
respect to the seasons we now experience. "Land of milk and
honey" symbolizes the love and wealth of Mother Nature.
Incidentally, our tiny friends, the bees, produce not only
golden nectar but also potent antibiotics and natural antisep-
tics in the form of propolis, pollen and royal jelly. A creature
feared by many is the snake. The king cobra is universally
respected as a most dangerous creature. As an illustration
of beneficence in apparently useless, menacing creatures,

research is revealing powerful healing qualities of venom which has been used successfully in the treatment of arthritis, muscular dystrophy, multiple sclerosis and polio, among other neurological malfunctions.

Slaughter is not justified by reason of satisfying the taste of the tongue, ornamenting and clothing the body, or making money. The dolphin certainly has more right to eat fish, which is its only food, just as the baby seal has a right to live beyond the first few weeks of its life, when savage butchering takes place in the name of fashion. Nature does not need human intervention to maintain her balance.

One who is entrenched in frantic activity (rajas) or the tamasic pollution of misconception cannot appreciate the merit of spiritual striving. The idea that the heart is more than a throbbing engine is alien. All perceptions become dulled with indulgence. Conversely, a sattva-permeated individual prefers satvic quality in food, environment and other beings. The predominant quality of a personality can be seen by the types of food eaten, speech and thoughts which are projected. Overcoming the three powers is facilitated by meditation, silence and constant vigilance. The conquest of lower tendencies must come before higher learning can occur. When one does not even practise simple things such as dietary discretion or refraining from the judgement of others, how can one expect further teaching and more intense sadhana?

The human being is basically a sensitive organism for the transmutation of energy. The more satvic one becomes, the more efficiently one holds satvic energy. The presence of High Beings purifies the atmosphere, temporarily lifting consciousness of those near. However, no being can give enlightenment to another, and higher teaching cannot be absorbed, understood or retained unless the human's nature is stabilized and purified. One cannot achieve a state of consciousness inharmonious with one's nature. One's nature is energy, elements of earth (vitamins, minerals, enzymes), air (oxygen), water (blood and lymph), and fire (energetic atoms and nerve impulses). Some seventy-two thousand channels lead from the solar plexus outward like the spokes of a wheel, connecting physical and subtle aspects of being. One is a vehicle of light. Consumption of vital elements in their purest state – focus of thought upon purity – can effect corresponding vibration within each cell of one's being. Blessed are those whose blood and judgement are so well commingled

In this fine, subtle state one attains Brahmacharya. That is, literally, living within Brahman, being one with the One. This involves the throwing off of wrong identity (duality) and retreating into the heart. The vow implies more than celibacy, for mind is the root of all sensuality. In order to realize Brahman within, one must abstain from all sense of indulgence. To fast whilst dreaming of the next meal is not fulfilment of the vow. Stimulating the emotions with the distractions of Maya (earthly sights and sounds) does not achieve the purpose. Brahmacharya implies discrimination. Even the most beautiful music, painting or poem, if used to arouse passion, is violation, wasted energy.

Focus must be upon spirit, which pervades all, attunement to the blissful symphony of Brahman, unaffected by frivolous distraction. Time and energy are devoted to contemplation and striving for samadhi, which is the holding of reality. The Brahmacharya does not thrill at the perfumery of illusion, does not eat to please senses but to nourish the castle of Brahman. Each thought, action and instinct is devoted as ritual to the highest goal. Even sleep becomes surrender to Source. When one tunes to That, lesser elements lose power. A vow is not meant to be worn as a badge, nor is it to be regretted once taken. Occasionally, a person will vacillate before taking a vow, saying "I'll try." This indicates one of two things: Either one still has desire for the thing disavowed or one does not realize the importance of sadhana. As Mahatma Gandhi wrote, " . . . where can be the difficulty in making the final decision? I vow to flee from the serpent which I know will bite me, I do not simply make an effort to flee from him. I know that mere effort may mean certain death. Mere effort means ignorance of the certain fact that the serpent is bound to kill me. That I could rest content with an effort only means that I have not yet clearly realized the necessity of definite action.... "

The green apple does not taste the same as the red, and neither red nor green is the taste of the yellow apple. What are colour and taste if not properties of energy? As vibrations of light through a prism transform into colour, differing waves of energy form taste. All apples are similar due to common qualities and components: minerals, enzymes, vitamins, carbohydrates, water and specific atomic structure of organized matter which separate them, for instance, from oranges. One may crave yellow vegetables for need of particular vitamins, or one may be getting the red signal. Beets, cherries, radishes, cabbage, tomatoes and watermelon may seem dissimilar, but all have antiseptic properties of the colour red. Green can calm nerves, both visually and when eaten. A room painted green soothes the eyes, creating an inner peace that is conducive to relaxation. Green vegetables do internal work through nerve-nourishing vitamins and minerals. The purpose of this colourful exercise is merely to illustrate that one is affected by seemingly insignificant nuances of energy. And then there are strawberries . . . which delight the heart.

Through attunement (at-one-ment) with Source, humans can effect evolution of higher consciousness throughout all levels of existence. This is actually the human being's responsibility as custodian of the planet. There was once a young Indian prince of superior intelligence and very fine sensitivity whose favourite pet was a lion . . . which the prince trained to be vegetarian. Now, it is commonly thought that vegetarianism is opposed to the nature of the lion-hearted, especially the beast itself. Perhaps this was a superior lion, but it is more likely that the animal responded to the power of enlightened love which reflected upon it. The energy of all spheres is improved by the purity of one soul and the fullness of one heart. One has oneself as the medium in which to paint one's rendition of the Source. AUM means 'yes' to the Highest, the opening of the heart to the Infinite.

5
Indra's Pearls

The greatest service you can give to the world
Is to take responsibility for yourself,
Your relationships and your environment.

SVAMI PŪRṆÁ

All things are interrelated, being manifold aspects of the One. Sri Aurobindo said, "Nothing to the supramental sense is really finite, it is founded on a feeling of all in each and each in all." Avatamsaka Sutra states, "The solid outlines of individuality melt away and the feeling of finiteness no longer oppresses us." Particularization, objectification, classification and duality per se are illusions of mind. Truth is defiled by the ego's desire for separate identity. Every action or thought of each single being creates a chain of repercussions involving others until eventually one's 'fate' has been experienced. Humanity may be regarded as one gigantic organism; movement of part affects the whole. Efforts of separateness by emphasis upon cultural, racial, sexual or religious differences must ultimately fail; unity is the truth of existence. If the world should suddenly fly apart, we would all go with it together, our apparent distinctiveness vanishing in flight. The deification of individuality at the risk of global health is indeed a socio-spiritual aberration. The law of compassion dictates the importance of world-wide co-operation and harmony. It means seeing in all other souls the reflection of one's own soul. This compassion is more than shedding tears over a sad movie or the misfortune of a friend. It is the ability to see beyond mental conditioning, bias and duality. The responsibility of the organism of humanity connotes mercy, understanding and straightforward dealings with all. There is a beautiful analogy in the imagery of Indra's glorious string of pearls. In one exquisite pearl in the chain shines the reflection of all the other pearls of Indra. When Jesus spoke, "I and my Father are one", he expressed the essence of compassion and the inner secret of genuine discipleship. It is not a material or gross surrender the Master requires, but profound identification with the Highest. Who is the Great Master? Atman, your own highest Self, which reflects within the glory of Brahman.

Scientific efforts to discover the true source of matter and isolate its smallest components, sub-atomic particles, have merely confirmed that the particles cannot be distinguished from the space surrounding them. They are observed to be probabilities – potentialities of manifestation in constant motion – sometimes appearing as particles and sometimes as waves of energy. They do not seem finite, but are properties of the mysterious Infinite. While they do not exist outside the dynamic, ever-changing activity of their field, they determine the quality of the space they inhabit. They appear to spring from the Void and cannot be isolated from one another, nor from the Void itself. It would seem that all matter is made of Nothingness – the Great Immeasurable. At the subatomic level, modern physicists have reached an echo of the macrocosm. To explain fully any phenomenon, one must explain all phenomena. For all is part of all else, connected by the very nature of being . . . ever-fluctuating, meshing, disintegrating, evolving energy. Indeed, only the mind creates separate, finite forms; the observer determines the observation. For every being on earth life is a continuous, rhythmic, dynamic transformation. Each infinitesimal particle of matter is in a state of constant change, well illustrated by Sivá's dance of creation, destruction and regeneration. There is unity and interdependence in all forms and events – as there is in karma.

Worldwide development, positive or negative, has its roots in collective karma of persons, groups and nations. The probability that an event will occur depends on this factor, though it would be unwise to assume that a particular development will definitely manifest. Karma is a complex network, involving desires, thoughts, actions, etc. of inter-relating beings, encompassing manifold lifetimes and interacting with other cosmic potentialities.

To estimate the course of a cart running downhill by consideration of weight, shape, gravity pull and angle of slope is possible, but still someone, somewhere may stop it or divert its route. Similarly one may be able to predict tendencies according to accumulated collective karma of the world population, but conditions may change instantly through the interference of global mass communication such as satellite assistance and computer back-up that may alter overall opinion. While reactions may vary as a result of group karmic influences, for example nationalism, special interest groups and cultural identification, generally people tend to imitate each other and are vulnerable to propaganda influence and media. The effect upon collective thinking influences not only the quality of life, but also the collective karma of the global village. Such effect may be positive or negative.

Technology appears to have reduced the spaces between us; is it possible that it will also accelerate time? Science has shown what ancient sages already knew: time and space are not separate, but depend upon one another and upon the being observing them – they are products of mind. Time flows at different rates in different places in space, depending upon the position of observation. Time also varies from place to place on earth itself. There are parts of the Himalayas where time stands still, so to speak. It is quite possible that the potential of an event may be brought into manifestation sooner or later in 'time', depending upon collective karmic influence. This explains partially the difficulty in giving precise predictions in terms of time – which is the bane of many a 'psychic'.

For some thousands of years now, earth and her inhabitants have been experiencing Kali Yuga, the age of iron, weaponry, industry, aggression, militancy, competition, anger, tension and gross materialism. Collective vision and self-image have become clouded with lust for power and object. As this delusion persists, the prognosis for positive planetary evolution is grim. Earth may be one of the smallest planets in the galaxy, but she has a special role in the cosmic system. She is said to be the only place where karma can be created and destroyed. She is the great instructress. How sad that the physical implements of her teaching are so often taken for the lesson itself. The magnificent fiery eruption of Mount St. Helens which recently devastated America's northwestern corner with the force of Vesuvius was a fine example of Kali power. She has spewed her ash over most of the continent and sent a volcanic cloud circling the globe. A once-beautiful emissary of nature, she suddenly blew off her top with five hundred times the energy witnessed at Hiroshima, as if to show the human impotence compared with nature's force. This tantrum could affect the weather in the entire northern hemisphere for some years with repercussions of drought, famine and flood, besides massive economic losses.

Her concussion flattened trees like matchsticks and created a moonscape out of one of the most beautiful areas on the planet. Of course, what first seems totally destructive behaviour on her part may have long-term benefits. Initially it was thought that she might usher in another ice age if her fuming were to continue with the same bulk of ash pouring into the atmosphere. Now she seems to have calmed somewhat to begin rebuilding her dome from within. She has provided scientists with an excellent natural laboratory for volcanic study. The very land she has demolished will now become, by her grace, more fertile and rich in minerals. In years to come the ash will decompose into life-giving soil as this illustration of creation/destruction/regeneration unfolds. Certainly it is of little use to curse God or to live in fear of the future. One must respect nature and study her lessons well, trying always to see beyond the obvious and to focus upon the positive aspects of every so-called adversity. Some people feel the vibrations caused by earth's movements, such as quakes and eruptions, and some are sensitive to weather phenomena, manifesting these effects with physical symptoms. If all that we on earth are dealing with is energy, is it not conceivable that, similarly, vibrations of human energy may in turn affect earth movement and the weather?

Contemplate upon the power of your own thought and emotion, upon the subtle effects you have on your own environment. Think of the responsibility of each link in a chain to maintain the strength and integrity of the totality. Remember Indra's pearls.

At this time the collective karma of the people certainly seems predominantly negative. Greed, lust, ignorance and all the various aspects of self-concern stemming from distorted ego are emphasized. On this basis destruction may very likely take place. Many believe the Kali Yuga will end in fire, sooner or later. But it has always been maintained by the Wise Ones of this world that:

> The positive defeats the negative,
> courage overcomes fear,
> patience defuses anger,
> love conquers hatred.

Accordingly, it is possible that the manifested positive strength of a few enlightened beings might prevent or delay disaster. You ask, "What is the use in delaying, if destruction will eventually come?" There is no use, unless the extra time is spent mindfully, so that evolution can occur.

With our actions and thoughts we eventually come to the end of our own determination. What one thinks one becomes, in this and subsequent lives. It is said that desires determine faith, faith determines acts, and as one acts one becomes, so long as one is in the 'bondage of karma, the forces of one's past lives'. This is the source of so-called fate, the sum of one's debts to nature. Karma is a law of sacrifice from which no one is exempt, unless and until liberation has been achieved. It is such a perfect system there is no need for intervention from the Highest. It has been said that God laid down the law and, as it were, retired. In view of the human's limited comprehension of the Limitless, it is best to accept the dictates of cosmic justice with resignation. We must pay all our debts to nature while under her rule. Every action has an equal and opposite reaction; it is imperative to be mindful so that confusion of thought does not create negative cross-currents. Even as one strives to achieve a goal one can set up one's own blocks through fear and doubt, thereby negating the positive striving in whole or in part.

Whenever you relate to someone or something, whenever you identify with a nation, group or race, you assume some of the inherent karma. The more intense or intimate the contact, the greater the accumulation of shared karma. Fervent espousal of any cause reaps the same harvest. For this reason one is wise to identify with God or guru. This means following the example, implementing the teachings in one's life. Identification is different from the projection of desires, which is negative and dangerous. One cannot manipulate God and the attempt can cause great harm. Within families, certain individuals often appear to have inherited physical or mental tendencies toward specific diseases. These proclivities can result from close mental or physical contact plus strong identification and affinity – as much the effect of shared karma as of genetic causes. Couples living together often come to resemble each other after some time. They may become so karmically attuned that they develop symptoms simultaneously, they actually share these physical manifestations even if separated by thousands of miles. When you have negative feelings toward anyone, you magnetically attract some of that person's negative karma, which then becomes your own. Hence the necessity of maintaining positive thoughts and feelings and identifying only with the One. It is essential to resist that seemingly universal human urge to criticize and condemn others, to succumb to jealousy, aggression and hostility. These block growth, instantly dragging you backward and further from the ultimate goal. Strictly speaking each negative impulse is a spiritual failure.

Every negative desire backfires, though only the most sensitive individual may be able to perceive the results. Many just go through life accumulating illness, phobias, incongruent ideas and confused emotional impressions, never stopping to wonder at the cause. Incidentally, the sadhana involving abstinence from all physical contact stems from the attempt to purify one's own karma without mixing energy and additional karma through touching others. There is more science to all of this than is usually assumed. In the karmic sense, physical contact can be the source of much psychic and emotional aberration. Living their lives as if immortal, most humans do not accept responsibility for their actions until noticeable deterioration and a variety of symptoms occur, until it is too late and 'life has cheated me', they say.

There is choice, which involves responsibility of the highest order. By changing yourself, you affect all who come into your contact. Many effects exist which are not 'seen'; but even if you pretend to say one thing with words there are many beings who can hear the truth of your feelings through the communication of energy. Even a flower will react whether your intention is negative or positive. That has been demonstrated scientifically. If flowers are so wise, can you expect humans to be less perceptive over what you try to hide? Contemplate, therefore, upon the positive quality of straightforwardness.

Purity of faith is the truest victory. The will of the cosmos is progress, not stagnation; movement rather than inertia. By believing in the constructive powers of nature, by sincerely feeling, "Thy will, not mine," and by accepting trials or misfortunes with resignation and profound humility, one may evolve. How can one reasonably dispute the justice of life when unable to remember one's own past life activity? In view of reincarnation, it is rather naive to blame those who by their actions repay one's former unkindness. They are merely playing out the karmic roles. One must not rely on one's own power alone, but must work in harmony with the cosmic will. Selfishness is the most unprofitable thing on earth: "What does a man profit if he gains the whole world and loses his own soul?" You might spend an entire lifetime trying to get something someone else has. That would be devotion to delusion. Growth will not result. One cannot fight cosmic law; there is no court of appeals and injustice is only a fault of human judgement. In the truest sense, one gets what one has earned.

A young Catholic priest, who was the epitome of vitality

and had many inspiring positive qualities, was struck down with terminal cancer. Grief-filled and horrified at God's iniquities, the members of his fold bemoaned the unfairness of it all, asking, "Father, why you . . . of all people surely you are the finest." "Why me?" the priest serenely answered, "Why not me?" The test of true faith is that it does not waver under the blows of adversity. Krishna said, "Having come to this world of sorrow, which is transient, love thou me. What seems at first a cup of sorrow is found in the end immortal wine. That pleasure is pure – it is the joy which arises from a clear vision of the Spirit."

Without belief we cannot grow. Self-limitation is the root of failure, for as we think we become. It is said that the sin is just missing perfection's target. An archer gains skill through aiming repeatedly at the mark, at first missing it a thousand times. In like manner, the fruit of sin – called punishment, misfortune or karma – perfects the skill of the seeker. Every problem can be taken as a challenge, another chance to grow. A warrior neither revels in nor curses fate but accepts each crisis as a step to climb towards the goal. Taittiriya Upanishad states, "If one places a gulf between oneself and God, this gulf will bring fear. But if one finds the support of the Invisible and Ineffable, one finds freedom from fear." Krishna said, "Be a warrior and kill desire, the powerful enemy of the soul. Set thy heart upon thy work but never upon its rewards. Work in the peace of yoga, free from selfish desires, moved neither by success nor failure. Yoga is evenness of mind – a peace that is ever the same."

One most insidious desire is the will to live, or fear of death. It is a form of duality, the very force which causes rebirth. In order to replace the transient with the Eternal, one must kill desire for individual everlasting life and merge fearlessly and totally with the Infinite. As long as one clings to the distorted belief of body being Self, death will be regarded with fear. Physical culture has been overemphasized to the detriment of other aspects of life. It is no secret that many would kill for knowledge of the technique to prolong youth. But what purpose is there in staying young and vital forever if the life is used wrongly? The spiritual message symbolized by the drink of immortality, distilled from the juice of the moon-blossoming soma fruit, is misunderstood by those locked in body-consciousness. Death is no less a natural transition than is birth. The butterfly's beauty is a consequence of the passing of one form. Should we assume it a great sacrifice on the part of the caterpillar? All matter is in a state of constant change. Why fear the inevitable? Movement is one more cosmic law; nothing in life is static; constant change and transformation are everywhere. The universe itself is moving non-stop . . . orbiting and simultaneously expanding at this very moment. How can one ever hope to hold on to a form? Nothing remains the same even for a fraction of a second. What power has illusion. In truth the boundaries between 'objects' and 'separate' beings do not exist outside of the mind, which creates and maintains the illusion. It has been suggested that the Gods conceal the happiness of death from humans, that they may endure life. This is not intended to inspire acts of suicide (which are ineffectual, in any case, for there is no escape from rebirth in that route). It is meant to remind us that life is not a playground but a medium of growth and learning. The only creature in the universe you can be certain of improving is your own self. Living is serious business, not a game of chance. Enlightenment does not fall from the skies – opportunity does not last forever.

The transient Manifestations of the One have no fundamental identity outside of the One, except in illusions of duality. Here lies the source of attachment, as told in the story of the yogi and the deer. A long time ago there was a sage who had withdrawn into the forest for the practice of yogic disciplines and spiritual meditation. One evening, as he was sitting by the banks of a stream, engaged in deep meditation, a lion's roar suddenly echoed through the stillness of the forest. The sound sent shivers of terror through a group of deer that had been grazing peacefully nearby. In their panic to escape the predator, the animals fled across the stream. Among them, however, was a pregnant doe who, unable to control the course of nature, gave birth just as she leaped . . . dropping the helpless fawn into the cold, rushing waters beneath.

The yogi, aroused from his meditation by the fearful vibrations of the herd, had witnessed the unfortunate birth and quickly rescued the newborn who soon recovered in the warmth and comfort of his arms. He took the young animal into his cottage and continued to care for it with great love.

As the days and weeks passed, the yogi's whole interest became centred on the little fawn. He developed such a great attachment to the little animal that he neglected all his practices, austerities and meditations. Then, early one morning, the deer wandered off into the forest and did not return all day. As the sun travelled through the sky the yogi's anxiety mounted, his anguish became so great that he completely lost his grasp on reality. He could not bear the agony of separation from the beloved deer and by nightfall the yogi lay dying . . . At that moment the deer returned, but it was already too late. With dying eyes the yogi beheld the lovely creature and there was sorrow in the heart of the deer.

This last impression was so strong upon both soul personalities that in their next lives the yogi incarnated as a deer, whereas the deer now had the human body of a sage who cared for the deer. It was in his life as a deer that our former yogi realized who he was. He understood that attachment was the sole cause of his present situation. In the light of this insight he waited for the natural destruction of his animal body, for further development to take place.

In their third incarnations after the incident by the stream, both soul personalities were human. The deer was now the yogi's father and both were gifted with the understanding of their karmic relationship. However, there were six other sons who did not share this wisdom. Their brother's quality of non-attachment was regarded as laziness and disinterest in anything they considered worthwhile. He was a constant source of aggravation to them. The brothers finally concluded that their sibling was good-for-nothing. In a last desperate attempt to let him be of some use, he was given the job to chase the birds off the fields. Surely he was able to do that. Alas, their reckoning had a flaw, for the yogi appreciated the opportunity of undisturbed meditation in the quiet fields and the birds happily picked the grain . . .

The enraged brothers had had enough. After giving him quite a useless lecture, they added an equally useless beating as a farewell and finally threw him out of the family for good.

Now our yogi was happy. Freed from all obligations towards the family, he was able to resume his spiritual practices. Once more he retreated to the forest life of his former incarnation, to austerity, peace and spiritual devotion. Henceforth he became a great sage, Jadabharata (Jada means like a tree and bharata is knowledge or wisdom). This name is quite descriptive, for he was a huge being, and like a tree, muscular and sturdy. Yet he had a rather peculiar walk, meandering, as if the legs were not connected to the rest of the body. It could be said that his head was in the trees, for he moved in a state of meditative quietude, far removed from the mundane thoughts of grosser men and women.

The ruler of the territory in which Sage Jadabharata moved was the great King Houn. For many years he had reigned wisely, bringing peace and prosperity to the land. Yet all his achievements had not brought him the fulfilment he yearned for. Disillusioned with life, his mind turned to spiritual matters. He decided that the time had come to look for his guru.

There was no time to lose. The bearers were called, the sedanchair prepared, and King Houn's venture into the jungle was mounted. This expedition in search of the guru, however, soon hit a snag when one of the king's bearers fell ill. Three men could not carry the sedanchair; a fourth had to be found quickly, but where? They were surrounded by jungle, far removed from human habitations. Nonetheless, a small party wandered through bush and brush in quest of a substitute. Finally they returned with a somewhat unusual fellow, Jadabharata, who agreed to take the job as the fourth bearer.

The journey continued, but the sage was an untrained walker, whose lack of skill resulted in a very bumpy ride for the king. His Majesty was not amused and scolded his men severely. The bearers, however, complained that the fault lay with this new man, who just could not keep in step and upset the balance. Jadabharata was duly reprimanded and again the party went forward. But every so often the sedanchair would wobble or take a strong dip as Jadabharata tried to avoid some small creature – insect and the like – upon the path. It was really too much to bear and the indignant king finally called a halt.

Angrily he shouted at his new bearer, "What do you think you are doing? I ordered you to walk properly, and you dare to disobey me? Do you realize who I am? I am the king. I can have you killed in a second . . . hanged . . . ", he really was quite beside himself.

Jadabharata calmly regarded the overheated monarch, "Who kills whom?" he replied. "You think you can kill me, but can you, really? What is it that you kill? You say that you are the king, but how do you know that? Who made you king, and what were you before you became king . . . ?" In this vein he proceeded to give the shocked and exasperated ruler a lecture the likes of which he had never had the good fortune to receive. Being himself no fool, King Houn recognized in this strange being, who dared to put the sovereign into his place without blinking a hint of fear, exceptional qualities and wisdom not found in the ordinary bearer. It must be added in the king's favour that he did attempt an apology, but this was met with more lecturing on the futility of apologies.

King Houn retreated into silence and awe at the realization that he had, indeed, found his guru. In this incarnation, therefore, Jadabharata's positive example of non-attachment inspired through constant communion with nature and spiritual devotion provided the opportunity for the king's spiritual growth. Remember Indra's pearls.

Indeed in every lifetime some opportunity for growth presents itself in various ways and forms. Prayer may herald and inspire such opportunity as in a prayer to Varuna, God of Mercy, from *Rig Veda*:

> 'We praise thee with our thoughts, O God.
> We praise thee even as the sun praises thee
> in the morning. May we find joy in being
> thy servants. You made the rivers to flow.

> They feel no weariness, cease not from
> flowing, but fly swiftly like birds in the
> air . . . May the stream of my life
> flow into the river of righteousness.
> Loose the buds of sin that bind me. Let not
> the thread of my song be cut while I sing;
> let not my work be ended before its ful-
> filment . . . we will now and evermore
> sing thy praises, even as they were sung
> of old – for thy laws are immutable, firm
> like the mountains.'

Something quite mystical happens when we pray, irrespec-
tive of which gods we choose to name. In the experience, an
unfoldment of Soul occurs and the individual's positive
energy is increased. In a sense, one's better side gains
strength, is brought to light. Any act of devotion sincerely performed exerts a positive influence upon the psychological
being. The valuable point, of course, is not whether God is
pleased that we kneel and pray, but rather that by visualising
God one becomes attuned to one's Higher Nature. Herein lies
an important secret of growth. Revelation of Spirit is like
unwrapping a beautiful present – as the twine is cut which
binds the mystery together, outer layers peeled away and
ornaments obscuring the treasure removed, light at last shines
upon the secret. When prayer and ritual have done their work,
they disappear and all that remains is the radiant jewel of
Truth.

Despite our spiritual potential, forecasts of gloom and
doom, whether volcanic, earth-rattling, celestial, economic or
political in origin, seem to abound these days. Regression
appears to have overtaken progress in areas of integrity,
ethics, spiritual compassion and altruistic feelings for other
inhabitants of Mother Earth. Fateful predictions which might
once have been considered absurdly unrealistic now cause
even the staunchest cynic to stop and think, if only for a
moment. The Goddess Kali can hardly be said to symbolize
harmony and sweetness, nor does the era bearing her name

signify an earthly heaven. It would seem that humankind now lives at the edge of drastic change; as global stress intensifies, the nuclear alternative seems 'just around the corner'. Separatist struggle and violence, engendered by poverty and emotional depression, is on the increase in the absence of overall peaceful coexistence and co-operation. Abuse of power and control in the hands of the privileged few, with no mind or respect for others, creates a general imbalance.

Symptoms of the disease of the planet are evident in its polluted waters and skies, its changing, unreliable weather conditions and the repercussions of drought and famine affecting so many forms of life. The realization of a nuclear war – the ultimate pollution – is unnecessary when our soil is quickly becoming the burial ground of chemical and nuclear waste.

And then there is the spiritual waste evidenced in an image of spirituality in which yoga means profit, power and prestige . . . religion is a business, and a pretence at being evolved is made in order to manipulate the ignorant. Only the truly evolved are able to help others uplift; you can only give what you have and there are no spiritual credit cards.

During the era of Mogul-reign in India, there was one emperor considered outstanding for his just and wise rule – Akbar the Great. Under his care the country's economy boomed and the arts flourished. Yet even the great Akbar's mind was shrouded in illusion, as this little anecdote illustrates.

Akbar the Great had been riding in the forests one day when his horse stumbled, threw him and left him lying injured and unconscious. The accident had occurred near a small cottage where a Spiritual Being lived. He found Akbar, took him home and in due time nursed him back to health. When the time came for the Emperor to leave, he revealed his identity and expressed his gratitude for the wonderful care he had received, " . . . and whenever you are near Delhi, please come to the court and I shall be delighted to receive you as my very honoured guest." With these words Emperor Akbar departed.

Time passed . . . until one day, on his way to Hardwar, the sage passed near the capital and thought it opportune to take up the Emperor's offer. He arrived at court, had his presence announced and waited. Finally Akbar appeared. The monarch was delighted to see the Being who had cared for him in his time of need. He apologized for having kept him waiting, explaining that he had been praying. "But now that you have come at last, allow me to make up for the selfless service you have rendered. Ask for anything you wish; if within my power, it shall be granted."

The Wise One contemplated in silence for a moment, then replied, "Tell me, when you were praying just now, what was your prayer, what were you trying to convey to the Almighty?" Akbar was surprised at this inquiry. "Well," he said, "I was asking God, who made everything so perfect for me, to please keep it this way – to continue giving me all the beautiful and rich things in life." The Spiritual Being nodded slowly, "So you were begging, in fact?" "Well, yes, I suppose I was," smiled the Emperor. At this the Being looked straight into the great Akbar's eyes and said, "One who begs himself, what can he give to others . . . ?" and he turned and left the palace.

The genuine seeker will eventually find the genuine teacher. He cannot be satisfied with any bogus replica. Yet even among the followers of a true emissary of Divine Light there may be those who long for fame, fortune and sex, who may try to manipulate and control, whose aim is not the enlightenment and growth they verbalize. They cannot, however, maintain their guise forever, for when the real work of self-discipline, honesty, and often painful self-analysis begins, they propel themselves out of the circle of true seekers by their own motivations, occasionally leaving a cloud of dust in their wake . . . .

Perhaps the passage of years will bring to earth a fresh start with a more highly evolved Being as her custodian – one who is excited by the creative potential of responsible thought and mindful action. The planet may be able to begin anew, but until then it helps little for those on earth to get depressed because of their stage of growth now. Time must not be wasted; the brightest compensation of Kali Yuga is the intensified challenge to those seekers who dare to oppose what to others seem insurmountable odds. In order to exist at the heights one must go beyond the superficial and be able to contemplate clearly the darkest depths. It is high time to grow. Krishna said, "Yoga is evenness of mind . . . if thy soul finds rest in me, thou shalt overcome all dangers by my grace. But if thy thoughts are on thyself and thou wilt not listen, thou shalt perish . . . for thou art in the bondage of karma, of the forces of thine own past life."

Death . . . Sacrifice . . . Sex . . . Love

Words exhibit a striking effect upon different people at different levels. Mere mention of the four nouns above probably evokes a more powerful chemical reaction felt physically, mentally and emotionally than any other words in the English language (money might be the fifth). The first two may produce a slight shudder while the last two cause much giggling and provide a financial bonanza for the entertainment industry. Sacrifice and death are linked in most minds as negatives, while the positives are felt to be sex and love, connoting a superficially romantic illusion of convenient pleasure. More profoundly considered, the first and third are closely related: the creative urge and the final expiration are opposite aspects of the same process. The sex act has been called the 'little death' and so-called death itself has often been described as the ultimate pleasure, transcendental euphoria. Sex is used by many people as an escape from 'real life', a sort of death. In its truest manifestation, love always involves sacrifice, for ego and even life itself are willingly surrendered. The real sacrifices of loving (with full consciousness) goes far beyond sexuality and is inherently a type of death which leads to higher existence.

If you regard yourself as a body, others will appear to you as bodies; all things in nature, plants, animals, people will be to you just objects and/or possessions. Some you will like, others you will dislike. You will use them according to your preference. It is easy to manipulate objects. And when you become ill or bored, you will refer to or blame another 'object' – God.

Spiritual growth requires a very different, truly loving approach as illustrated in the relationship of Yajnavalkya and Maitreyi.

Yajnavalkya told his wife, Maitreyi, it was time for him to settle his possessions with her and retire to a life of meditation. She objected, "What should I then do with possessions that cannot give me life eternal? Give me instead your knowledge." He answered, "Dear you are to me, beloved, and dear are the words you say . . . hear my words with deep attention. In truth it is not for the love of a husband that a husband is dear, but for the love of the soul in the husband that a husband is dear. It is not for the love of a wife that a wife is dear, but for the love of the soul in the wife that a wife is dear. It is not for the love of children . . . of Gods . . . of creatures . . . it is the soul, Spirit, the Self, that must be seen and be heard and have our thoughts and meditation, O Maitreyi. When the soul is seen and heard, is thought upon and is known, then all that is becomes known."*

Indeed it is in circumstances of major challenge and difficulty that the real opportunity for growth is found. In the 16th century, the great philosopher/physician Paracelsus wrote, "The highest foundation of medicine is love" and "I do not know where I shall have to wander now, I do not care either, as long as I have helped my sick." Obviously, this sort of love had little to do with convenience and a lot with sacrifice. Appearing more a vagabond than the erudite doctor he was, and in the face of great hardship, Paracelsus revolutionized medicine, laying the foundation for all of modern natural science, methodical research, psychological healing and pharmacology. His miraculous cures, holistic philosophy and courage brought him notoriety as a sort of magician and soothsayer. His knowledge came from diverse and unusual observations gathered during extensive travel – from being captured by Russian Tartars and initiated into Shamanism, to studying at leading institutions of his time. He wrote, "It is indeed possible for man to get hold of and to enclose the whole

---

* From *Brihadaranyaka Upanishad*

of the world in his grasp and this with all its foundations and in clear perspective of its perfect entirety." With dedication and a fierce will that could not be broken, he demystified some metaphysical concepts while also uncovering greed and quackery among his colleagues. Standing alone against the 'medical corporation' he suffered derision and utter humiliation from the other scholars and doctors. He was forced to endure financial ruin. Experimenting on himself in the name of research, he eventually ended his life. Today his ideas have acquired influence in medical science. He might be called the father of homeopathic medicine as well as experimental research.

Savitri, inspiration, shines through the examples of this life of sacrifice and dedication to Higher Love. As is written in *Rig Veda*, "Let our meditation be on the glorious light of Savitri. May this light illumine our minds." Savitri sent the mind and its powers to find Truth. By the grace of Savitri our mind is one with him and we may strive with all our power for light . . . leading our thoughts to heaven – he gives everyone their work.

Paracelsus endeavoured to cure the body while never losing sight of reality beyond the physical realm. Studying nature's mysteries and sharing that knowledge was more important to him than the comfort and material security he sacrificed. Through the strength of his faith man stands above the (lower) spirits and overcomes them. The following were his "Five Entities" from which all diseases, physical and mental, derive:

1. disharmony in the human's own body (physical deterioration and abuse)
2. environmental harm (wrong food, polluted air and water, lack of exercise, smoking, drugs, etc.)
3. mental discrepancies, dangerous biases and suggestions (negative thought, conditioning and over-emotionalism, living in fantasy)
4. corrupted influences of the world-soul (this is where collective thought and collective karma come in)
5. divine wealth and judgement (karma). The result of wrong thought, wrong speech and wrong action.

In today's circumstances we would all do well in learning to read and understand the 'signature of things', as he would have put it, that meaning of life which is more than skin deep. It is fairly easy to feel proud of the accomplishments of the world's great ones – harder to see one's own reflection in the negative acts of others. Every being is responsible for the environment and has effect upon others. Remember the pearls of Indra. Contemplate upon that image the next time you feel a karmic attack or negative impulse. Learn to feel joy in the happiness of others; savour their growth and success as if it were your own victory. Rejoice for others, and your compassion will reflect upon your own higher growth, bringing you closer to the Ultimate Truth.

6

Soham . . . I am That

But know that, by which all is pervaded,
to be imperishable.
No one can bring about the destruction
of this immutable principle.

BHAGAVAD GITA

Every creature feels the urge to grow, perpetuate and evolve. This is governed by instinct and senses as well as cosmic law. Senses pleasure a being and lead it to the source of the enjoyment if intelligence is involved. Unfortunately many humans use up entire lifetimes seeking sensual pleasures rather than finding the true source of bliss. The senses are just a spark of the totality which creates them. They give a hint of the extreme delight one finds when merging into the Infinite. How sad that so many are fascinated by the spark that they fail to reach the eternal flame. High Beings will not suggest that one should renounce the senses but transform them into higher energy so that one grows through them rather than being bound by them to a lowered state of consciousness. The idea is to master the mind, body and senses, not to be victimized by them. One comes to use every part of one's being for higher growth, changing that which stands in the way. When one has self-control, no one can provoke, tempt or rouse one to anger; one is no longer driven away by the wild horses of the senses nor by the manipulative efforts of others. If one decides to do something, one does it without being swayed by anyone or anything, including one's own wayward senses. One is in command, realizing that the physical body is a transitory vehicle given for use in growing on the earthly plane. Nothing less, nothing more. If one can discover cosmic law which leads to bliss and live by that, one will achieve the purpose of life. If one chooses human 'law' and ignores the truth, one will destroy oneself. The five senses try to enslave so that one expends all one's energy trying to fulfil their desires. But when one's real centre is found one is able to use all aspects of oneself as tools to fit one's purpose.

Life is like a bubble which is formed and destroyed. The purpose of this cosmic play is to find one's root or centre . . . the cosmic Self which is indestructible. The personal units of life appear merely for an instant upon the spacescape of the universe. We are, all of us, ephemeral forms of energy descended from the first molecules of life which emerged from the cosmic swirl over four billion years ago. Like Indra's pearls, double strands of DNA spiralled their genetic code to form the first particles of earthly matter so long ago that our human minds cannot imagine. Each molecule of DNA holds as many atoms as a galaxy has stars; every living cell evolved from that seed. An individual human is composed of trillions of cells, a universe in itself. One is in fact a multitude. A congregation of minuscule creatures lives within the body's environment. Actually, if one could just see those tiny fellows who travel the length and breadth of the eyelashes one would be amazed. These beings exist in unimaginable profusion; and one thought one was alone . . . a distinct, unique and solitary person! It is quite a responsibility to house such a voluminous group. To them the human is God . . . the source of life.

The human being considers itself the gem of creation, and this might be the potential but the model does not seem to be complete. Something has gone amiss; the arrogance is not justified. In the name of progress individuals, groups, societies, cultures, communities, nations, etc. strive towards material success, creating a plethora of goods and services to make life more convenient and pleasurable. The marketplace is filled with the products of material dreams; even people are offered as commodities. True devotees of materialism do not believe in myths or gods but are conditioned to accept only that 'reality' they can touch or feel. They see the surface of life and try to negate anything deeper than the most immediate concerns of the senses.

Many seem to think that science has all the answers and with enough research all the questions of the cosmos will be solved by God-science so that life will be (almost) perfect. Actually, perfection is not a real goal to the materialist, who believes in compromise. Humankind waits for science to make everyone happy; rich and healthy. Meanwhile life grows further out of balance. Time may run out. The economy might fail. There might not be enough money for research to continue its quest. Of course, the material world has its uses. Indeed there is no more valid medium for manifestation of spiritual growth and evolution than the blue planet earth; it is no coincidence that this small globe is coloured with the hue of the Infinite. In fact, the possibilities of material development are endless. Over the millenia, humankind has selected which beings in the animal and vegetable kingdom it preferred. They flourished or dwindled often through deliberate hereditary encouragement of the human will. As the human mind has focused, so life has manifested. Earth always reflects the consciousness of her custodians. That is not coincidental, though blatant materialists would seek to disavow any responsibility.

In these circumstances people should realize that the greatest service to be given to the world is to take responsibility for oneself, one's environment and one's relationships. Individual creative intelligence is vital to be free of the misconceptions others try to impress. To go beneath surface appearances in order to see beyond previous conditioning and biases one must be firm in the resolve to grow and realize at all times that ego should not stand in the way of growth by such tools as worry, depression, anger, doubt and envy. Constant vigilance is required for people to channel this force productively.

Long before the age of technology the forces of nature were worshipped. People felt reverence for the life-sustaining qualities of sun, moon, trees, oceans, rivers, etc. It was considered a sin to cut the trees or to soil the water; pollution was a crime at that early point in human development. What right do we have to spoil the mountains, disturb the natural balance of the earth, cause soil erosion and depletion of soil's fertility by thoughtless acts? Mother Earth is there for us to love – a nourishing, nurturing and generous mother. Do you ruin your house with a slovenly and neglectful attitude, or do you preserve and enjoy that environment as if it were a reflection of you? Do you also care responsibly for the bodily shell which houses your spirit, focusing on health and cleanliness rather than mere vanity? Is your mind filled with negativity and anxiety or does it reflect purity, balance and wisdom? Perhaps it is time to surrender your confusion to a higher guide that is not blinded by ego or intellectual maelstroms . . . infinite consciousness is never closed to anyone. Yoga can be the key.

There are numerous misunderstandings about that term, Yoga. Some think it is like a sport by which the body is built and the sensual nature is sensitized. Others see it as a religion or a strange practice from the East that turns normal Westerners into fanatics. Yoga is a scientific method by which one grows physically, psychologically and mentally into a more complete human being. The term, pronounced 'yog', means literally: union, harmony, completeness, poise, wholeness. It is derived from the word 'yoke' and denotes harnessing the various aspects of an individual into a dynamic vehicle of evolution. Yoga creates a powerful totality within the life – balance – instead of fragmentation and weakness of will. It can intensify the integrity of a being, lead to fulfilment and strength of character. Yoga leads to revelation of the inner Self, which is immortal. Yoga can be the master key to the door leading to bliss.

By now most have come to understand that misery may occur in any circumstance. Rich and poor alike share in suffering. All the powers of the world will not give peace, spiritual stability or contentment. One can have all the wealth and all the people in the world on one's side and still be unhappy. Every being hopes to reach fulfilment but most are locked in illusion, thinking that this thing, place, person, work or luxury will satisfy the need. It is a great illusion to seek happiness outside oneself; the individual is the real cause of his or her own suffering. Maya's subtle play reflects everywhere in the marketplace. "See this . . . see that . . . try me . . . eat this . . . experience that . . . here's something you need . . . just what you have been looking for . . . " All is illusory and the happiness disappears as soon as it has been tasted or touched. As one reaches for the beautiful house, the delicious food, the wonderful friends, the entrancing movies or music, gold, diamonds, etc. the sense of fulfilment vanishes. These are phantoms, shadows of an ever-changing whim and desire. They do not last; the substance dissolves. Senses can never give the fountain of bliss that is craved. 'Fun' is not the purpose of life. Instead one should evolve through experiences and make use of every moment to further growth. In particular, money has become a form of energy to be used or abused. It can be used to build, to help earth's inhabitants, or it can be abused and thrown away on negativity.

Sadly, many people spend their lives as if they will live forever, as if the savings account will build up enough interest to ensure immortality. It does not work that way. At the door of death, many see the waste.

Life is the given vehicle that one may learn the mysteries of life. If the task is not completed in the allotted time, nothing can be done. There is no use regretting the inevitable. Every moment of life can be turned into sadhana, an exercise for growth. Whatever one does, how and where one walks, each thing eaten, all the words spoken, the way in which one works or relates to the people in one's sphere – everything can be instrumental to growth. The problem is that most people are not willing to 'give up' anything in order to achieve the Infinite, which is intangible. It seems a great gamble. How can they turn their backs on all the temptations which seem so real? What would happen if everyone renounced? Would we still have wars; would people in 'underdeveloped' countries still be starving while those in 'developed' countries try to figure new ways to lose weight without giving up gluttony?

In ancient India there was a king who renounced all and became a great yogi. One day as he tried to meditate, desire took precedence over his efforts. He had the urge to eat something sweet. He thought that if he suppressed the temptation it would just lie dormant to arise again at another time. So he left meditating and went to the market where he worked all day for a man who owned a sweet shop. At the day's end the yogi was given his payment in the form of sweets. These he took back to his place of meditation at the bank of a river. He proceeded to devour the delicacies, which his mind and senses enjoyed. The first he ate tasted very delicious so he tried a second, third and fourth. At that point his mind informed him, "I am satisfied, thank you; I have had sufficient sweets." The yogi replied, "No, I am not yet finished. You must have more of what you desired so strongly." Mind said, "How can I? I'll have the rest tomorrow." "No, you will have them all now," said the yogi, continuing to eat. Finally mind and body could not stand any more of that and with great resentment forced the yogi to regurgitate. That which he vomited he again ate, forcing himself again and again. Mind said, "Never will I care for sweets again. Never will I demand or desire that which is unreal." While such rigorous methods are not for everyone, a steady resistance against mind's many tricks will eventually yield lasting results. In order not to be deceived by the mind, ego and emotion, one needs strong thought, wisdom and knowledge. People must learn to grow through and beyond the desires which may ground them.

The mind is very active. It takes the body and creates pain. If one is hurt one feels something intense, possibly throughout the entire body, like a chain reaction. It hurts to the very centre. Because one becomes angry at the hurt, one's disposition changes radically. The suffering motivates one to act in strange ways; depression, frustration, revenge, even suicide can ensue. The blame is placed outside oneself . . . the world is unfair. People create their own pain by being neglectful and disrespectful of their bodies, by overdoing things, by fighting with others, etc. The mind can create and control many aspects of one's life. It should not be confused with the intellect, or buddhi, which is more neutral; the mind is biased, it thinks only of its own wishes, not of the well-being of others. It is self-centred.

Ahamkara, the lower or ego-mind, is a rascal, a crooked,

selfish entity. Whereas the higher mind is determination and reason. It is notable that sometimes one cannot solve a problem until one 'lets it rest' awhile, 'sleeping on it' or diverting attention; then the answer comes miraculously. When water is poured into a pot, it may take some time for the particles in it to settle down to the bottom, at which time the water is very clear. It is the same with solution-hunting. If the mind and intellect are both actively involved, one might look forever and not be able to see clearly. But once the mind settles down, intellect is able to provide the solution. One might call that intuition or right tuning. As with radio frequencies, sometimes there is a disturbance on the band; the long wave can come in clearly so that it is easier to communicate from the north pole to Argentina than from Britain to France. Although a gross example, this is how the mind works.

When a master trains a disciple, there is eventually no more verbal communication. Time and distance no longer matter. It can happen that the disciple is ten thousand miles away and the teacher is able to communicate very clearly. It can also happen that the disciple is sitting next to the teacher and no communication takes place, no matter how hard one tries. If the frequency is very powerful and high, the message is clear. In mountainous areas television and radio reception is poor; in an airplane the signals are more easily received. When there is disturbance in the air the messages do not come through. The success of satellite communication is an example of the efficiency of very high tuning which is not bound by the usual obstructions of earth's gravitational atmosphere. With clarity and calming of mind, also, communication becomes easier. The capacity to relate becomes greater at certain heights, psychologically as well as spatially. Just as a camera focused on a close-up shot sees only part of a thing, the farther from the object it gets, the more complete the viewpoint becomes.

The intellect is not under the influence of the mind. Its job is to analyze and then to submit its report to the mind, which is supposed to follow its advice. Intellect represents the 'wife' who tells her 'husband', mind, what is right. But mind is such a bad husband that he ignores the wisdom of his wife, listen ing instead to his own fantasies and previous conditioning. The results are usually negative. There is a play of four entities involved in this drama, and they are the best actors and actresses in all creation. The second couple are the female, emotion, and her husband, ego. These two cannot live without each other. Sometimes ego comes from emotion, and at other times emotion is derived from the workings of ego. They are always inseparable and very persistent. In fact, even when one leaves the physical body the two couples will remain in the form of one's subtle body, which is the mediator or 'transformer' between two other entities, the cosmic Self, or Atma, and the physical body.

The body moves exactly as the mind wishes, being its servant. It has been said that flesh is dumb. The body is like an empty vehicle with no reality of its own, pulled by ten wild horses, driven by the mind, although the true owner is hidden somewhere else. Of the four aspects, two are positive when not influenced negatively by their partners. When intellect and emotion are transformed, they can create positivity in mind and ego. The whole drama is dominated by ego and emotion; they act, feel, do, experience, move, talk and react. Most of humankind's performance involves either ego or emotion, who have stolen the stage so powerfully that many people forget the other players exist. One must develop neutrality in order to avoid seeing everything through the perspective of these two. One should not identify with ego, not allow emotion to carry away reason.

One way to remain clear is to identify with everything outside oneself. When looking at water, experience the water as oneself. If one sees a bird, feel that bird. Really understand how connected people are to trees, plants and clouds . . . to the planet Mars, Mercury or the Moon. The other way is not to identify with anything. The problem is that humans choose to identify with some things and not with others, liking and hating. They are caught in a trap of duality, missing the unity through the opposites that blind them. How wise is Maya! One must work very hard for Self-knowledge.

In the *Bhagavad Gita*, Arjuna breaks down in the midst of battle saying, "I don't understand." He is ready to give up, run away, escape his problems. He asks Krishna, who represents Paramatma, to show him the way out. Jivatma-Arjuna does not want to do anything, wants to leave the cares of life, does not want to conquer, fight, become a king, be a great warrior, enjoy control and power . . . he wants nothing. Krishna said, "Where will you go? There is only one way out." He is like a man caught in a huge maze, a forest with only one road leading out. When finally he sees the way, he decides to walk past it like a blind man. Then he has to go all around the maze again. There is only one way to evolve, but as soon as the path is shown, the being does not want to see it. That is the work of ego and emotion, they are both very strong adversaries to growth who hide the way so that one becomes ensnared in the illusions of Maya like a spider caught in its own web. It is like the monkey who gets his hand stuck in a pitcher full of something he desires such as peanuts. If only he resists the delicacy and lets his fist open he is free; otherwise he gets neither the nuts nor his freedom. The moment one gives up ego and ego-centred emotion one frees oneself.

In milling grain it has been the custom in India to cover the eyes of bulls so they do not know they are going around in circles hour after hour. Otherwise they would not move. The bull likes to wander around in freedom. When his eyes are closed he feels he is covering many miles of territory, imagining himself a great traveller. In a similar illusory darkness some people think they are bound by destiny, that they cannot get loose from the dictates of fate. Arjuna thinks he cannot possibly get out of his problem, it is too huge. Krishna tells him it is only a question of leaving illusion – ego identification and ego desires which lead Arjuna in circles. Emotions form fantasies that are counter to growth. One must be vigilant to overcome such tricksters within one's own personality. It is such a mistake to imagine that the enemy is outside the self. One is one's own enemy when one refuses to see beyond one's own ego – when living a fantasy rather than reality.

In a small village a man stands at a riverside watching a cargo boat full of cotton float by. He then goes home and has a 'heart attack'. A doctor is called to treat this man who is a cleaner of cotton by profession. The doctor finds the heart in good shape, and no apparent reason why the symptoms should have occurred. But since he dabbles in psychology the doctor decides to look deeper for answers to the mystery and asks the man where he went, what he saw and did that day. In talking the doctor mentions, "Did you happen to hear about the huge load of cotton that burned today on the river?" The sick man becomes very excited when he hears that. He is suddenly cured. "Is it true . . . really? It burned? Oh, thank God!" Seconds earlier he was drifting off to death at the prospect of cleaning all that cotton. He had thought, "In this village I am the only one who knows how to clean the cotton," With the destruction of that responsibility his health problem also vanished miraculously.

Whatever pictures are created in the mind become the foundation of the life. They are laid down, one after the other, over the years until they form a hardened shield of misconception, somewhat like earth that forms striations over long periods of time, layers in rock. All together that is what is called samskaras and karma, which bind. These layers must be removed and unfolded one by one through the dramas of life. One is conditioned by one's karma. It all seems very real, unbreakable, fate. Anything outside that prison seems unattainable. Many religions support that illusion by teaching that it is impossible to attain the Infinite . . . that no one can be perfect. That is not true. If one can create, one can also destroy, in a positive sense. One can find out who and what one really is, beyond one's fantasies and egoistic imaginings. One holds oneself prisoner and can set oneself free. As Krishna explained to Arjuna, "What you think is real is only a reflection of your own illusion." These problems that seem so great do not exist. Fantasy and imagination can seem the very basis of one's life. They are difficult to give up. The mind has solidified illusions, the ego has fixed the mould of misconception, and emotion has made the mixture even stronger, like cement with water added to it. One is stuck. One's very essence becomes disturbed on all levels.

The word friendship is often misused. How many true

friends do people have? Are they good friends to themselves? If not, then perhaps they are not friends to others, either. In a profound sense, Krishna and Arjuna are friends, yet they are not on the same level. Arjuna relates to Krishna on the human level rather than on the divine level. That is his problem. He is limited by a human perspective, he cannot see the whole story. When Arjuna is incapable of communicating with Krishna he becomes very frustrated and angry. This story, which takes place on the battlefield, is a dialogue between an individual soul, Jivatma, and the totality, Paramatma. The warrior confides his confusion to God, who neither opposes nor accepts but patiently listens, hoping his friend will come to understand. The gap between them is huge. It is not the warrior who rises to the level of the Divine but the higher who goes to the lower in order to teach. There is no obligation in true friendship but Arjuna gets upset when he feels Krishna does not take his problems seriously. It is very human to get so involved and confused that the problem grows far beyond its real size. Krishna feels no pity at all for Arjuna's plight, for he sees that the warrior can grow out of his delusion. But it can be frustrating when your companion and friend takes everything differently. Arjuna must break the boundaries of human limitation he has set for himself. From the human point of view Krishna might seem cruel. What Arjuna experiences as cruelty is something different from the standpoint of Krishna, whose knowledge and vision are greater.

The important thing is to tune to cosmic consciousness and experience that divinity, breaking through the limits of human mentality. So Arjuna tries hard to overcome human attachment and instinct and Krishna serenely watches his manifestations of human consciousness, letting him speak and speak until he can speak no more. At last, in exhaustion and desperation, Arjuna cries out, "I'm a coward, lost. My nature is corrupt. I do not know good from bad, right from wrong, where to go, what to do. My mind and intellect are distorted, I am living in darkness. Please, O Lord of Dharma, lead me whatever way is right. I am not at the point of decision-making. I surrender myself to you, I become your disciple . . . show me the way." He did not say, "I am your friend, therefore you should help me." He realized then that he was not an equal to Krishna, who was not blinded by Maya. To such high beings Maya becomes subject, not ruler. Krishna was not Arjuna's friend on the level of illusion, but he was a more profound friend, the higher Self. Atma is a reflection of that Self on the individual level. It is that Self which utterly prevails. In all relationships one must strive to manifest that higher aspect. Then mothers, fathers, brothers, sisters, friends and all other beings contacted in life are no longer seen as objects apart but as reflections of the same Atma one shares. It is the divinity in each which one responds to, not the various qualities of duality. The Infinite does not see in terms of race, sex, nationality, religion or other superficial distinctions. It is the totality of life, one's true meaning and essence. Atma is within you and within all others which appear to be separate from you. That is a good thing to contemplate.

One of the highest states of being is that consciousness in which nothing matters, not in the negative sense of Arjuna's confusion, but as with Krishna. It is like the beautiful sandalwood forests in India. Their fragrance is so delightful that many snakes are attracted. But the trees stand aloof, impervious to the poison and slithering desires of the serpents. In the same way, those who have developed the ability to manifest the Self are not touched or influenced by surrounding negativities, accidental or intentional. Arjuna asked how one with mental stability behaves. Krishna said, "He may behave like the ordinary human, may do everything – walk, talk, act; still he is not involved in the performance of acts. He constantly maintains a higher state of consciousness."

Anyone can attain peace and stability. It is a matter of saying to oneself, "I am not going to let this affect me, it will not last forever, it is a passing phase, this is not what I really am." When one has the knowledge of what one really is, one can maintain happiness regardless of circumstances, despite outside difficulties and tests. If one remains mindful and does what is required there will be no reason to regret or be dissatisfied. There is nothing to blame or dispute. If one has done the correct thing, has acted positively, there will be no need to worry. Do only two things: that which is necessary and the Ultimate. Do not bother with the rest. One should be totally real and not identify with any role played in life.

One is something beyond any of the classifications others may have. One should give what is needed and not get attached to anything. As one relates to family, friends and associates, remember to relate fully and truly. The sun's rays hit the various aspects of the earth at different angles and serve different purposes, such as creating clouds from water, warmth and foodstuff to nourish plants, dryness for the earth, energy for life and growth. It is always the same sun falling on a house, a lawn, a tree or a body. It cannot be thought of as more or less sun. Love is like that. In love one does not give less or more, one identifies with the Atma in all. One does not use sensual whim or distorted preference in love, for instance loving one child more because its eyes are blue or its personality is reminiscent of someone. That is illusion, not love. One loves the children because they, too, are Atma. Together, all are part of the Infinite and that is a beautiful thing to feel. It is the same with friends. One should respect the Atma in all rather than feeling competition and envy.

The prescription for attainment of stability has been stated frequently but will be repeated here: meditate, contemplate, relax, breathe deeply, be careful of diet (choosing only pure and fresh foods), be vigilant of ego and emotional states which can drag one down; avoid excitable and negative tendencies, places and people; be careful of one's own thoughts and speech. If the three strands of materiality (the gunas) are not harnessed they will lead one into chaos and sorrow. When one has purified one's nature – mind, body and soul – one will not be the puppet of sensual desires. Then one will be free to grow further, into more subtle realms of reality. Unless one is able to take the first steps to sacrifice one's animal nature nothing will change. Food, sex, sleep and fear are energies that humans have in common with animals. Unfortunately most are dominated by these forces with little balance or restraint. Perhaps one starves oneself, then the mind is unstable due to lack of proper nutrients; or one eats too much (that is a disease) and again the mind and spirit are affected adversely. In sleep one either does not get enough rest or one sleeps too long, only to awaken enervated, or uses sleep to escape life. One may be frozen by fear of losing, of being humiliated or insulted, of dying, of disease, of not being loved and accepted by others. Sexual energy is creative energy. It can be wasted thoughtlessly or transformed into spiritual power. To save this energy and direct it positively means life, while misuse leads to suffering. A wheel needs a central point of contact, an axis, in order to turn and spin. One never loses touch with one's central point – the spine – as one moves through life.

But society today has lost that core. It has no idea where it is going. Therefore there are many theories around which are simply erroneous. Psychiatrists believe that one must release sexual tension or one will become neurotic. It is true that suppression and regression can be unhealthy. The idea is to use contemplation, analysis and right thought to control the mind so that the sensual thoughts do not arrive in the first place. Tantra, which is a philosophical and psychological system dealing with the energy circuits of the human body, has little to do with sex, although that aspect of it has been sensationalized by the non-evolved who are always looking for new techniques of satisfying sensual indulgence. Tantra utilizes sexual energy by transmuting it to spiritual energy; by opening chakras – energy 'wheels' – creative intelligence is enhanced. Through discipline and by understanding the truth behind human instinct one is able to stop sensual thoughts from manifesting. Prana, life force, is preserved and used for higher growth. One who lives by animal functions has no need to preserve prana. As Krishna said, "One who dwells on sensual pleasures creates desire for them, first feeling attraction and then the lust for possession. This leads to passion and anger. From this comes confusion of mind, then loss of discrimination and reason, and loss of reason leads to destruction. There is no wisdom for one without harmony and balance, and without that there is no contemplation, no peace, no joy . . . Passion carries away wisdom even as the wind drives a vessel on the waves." There remains one further consideration: shared intimacy of any kind will also produce equally intimate karmic interaction.

There is much to learn from myths of High Beings, if one can divorce one's perception from the desire to view everything through the murky filter of the senses. Look beyond the surface to understand meanings symbolized, for instance, in the stories of Krishna, the Lord of Lords of Yoga. It is limiting to think of him as a human being. He was an avatar of Vishnu, the Preserver of the Universe, and he often used the elusive Maya as a tool. He could change his form at any time and he played tricks on people in order to shake up their sleepy consciousness, removing ego and body consciousness so that cosmic, or Krishna consciousness could emerge. The pranks of the boy Krishna were actually tests and trials to break the hardened shell of conditioning. He was a beautiful manifestation of illumination and everyone who met him fell in love with his perfection. Like so many ancient myths of various cultures, the story of the divine child began with immaculate conception as Vishnu decided to begin a new incarnation of himself . . . as if to suggest that we are self-perpetuating beings.

Such stories are illustrations of the mysteries within all beings. They are a kind of blueprint for the evolution of consciousness. At the roots of every religion, including Hinduism, Christianity, Islam, ancient Egyptian belief and the Chinese cults of the Mother, lies the Self-determined birth – God creating and recreating Itself, self-sacrifice and rebirth. These aspects of divinity must be accepted as important values of the human collective consciousness which created the myths. The point of focus is transformation, giving birth to one's real Self and sacrificing those aspects which obstruct growth. The importance of symbolism should not be underestimated. Some of the most profound myths are shrouded in symbolism.

These myths are not simple dramas, romances and tragedies like those seen on television or in film. To view them superficially is to miss the point entirely. All the characters are aspects of oneself, waiting to start one's personal drama of evolution, so they can play their roles. If one never seeks to grow, is unwilling to sacrifice any part of oneself to evolution, these inner actors will be denied their chance to perform. Waiting forever in the wings of one's consciousness, they become frustrated and angry. Consequently, they can wreak havoc upon one's life . . . destroying with a vengeance. Hell has no fury like the repression of growth. Since these deities exist within, meditation and contemplation will help them emerge faster than anyone explaining their meaning. The only way to assimilate the deeper truths held within the myths, is to look into oneself. Perhaps some guidepoint can help one get started though. The symbolism of the moon is a dominant theme in countless religions. The early worship of Mother Earth and the Cosmic Mother included such deities as the Virgin Mary and the Black Goddess at Mecca (a Kali figure). The Vedas often refer to the moon as the source of soma, the fruit of immortality. The Latin word for mind stems from moon and, of course, one is familiar with the words 'lunar' and 'lunacy'. Some connection would be suggested between the sun's mirror and one's own mind. This is a good thing to contemplate. Perhaps the source of immortality is within. Do not be frightened; contemplation will not turn someone into a lunatic, but it might lead to a more enlightened state.

There is quite a complicated story regarding Krishna's birth. When Vishnu decides to incarnate himself in another form, as Krishna, he goes to the underworld (unconsciousness) to place himself in six embryos, which are demons sleeping beneath the earth. The king of that time, Kamsa, has been told that he will be killed by the eighth child born to his cousin Devaki. Therefore he decrees that all Devaki's children will be killed at birth. Vishnu infuses the six demons with his breath, thus killing the evil in them, and tells the goddess Sleep to place them in the womb of Devaki. He also promises Sleep that she will become goddess of the world for this deed. The seventh of Devaki's embryos becomes Krishna's brother, Balrama, also called 'Samskarama', the 'Plougher of Samskaras'. This embryo is transferred by miscarriage in the seventh month to the womb of the constellation Rohini, beloved of the moon.

It is interesting to note that Krishna's brother is described as luminous with the pale beauty of the cool-rayed orb . . . and this moonlike incarnation of Vishnu is connected by name to the eradication of samskaras, those conditioned tendencies which bind us. Vishnu places the eighth part of himself in Devaki's womb, while Sleep is placed in the womb of Yashoda, the cowherd Nanda's wife. When both children are born simultaneously in the eighth month, after the death of the first six newborns, the infants Krishna and Sleep are switched. As King Kamsa attempts to kill Sleep by throwing her upon the ground, she leaves her body and flies to the heavenly abode of Kali. She is adorned with the wealth of Lakshmi and the beauty of the moon. From her station above the earth the four-armed goddess (signifying the four phases of the moon) calls to Kamsa with a voice of thunder and doom. The king hears her as his own death. Meantime, Vishnu has successfully recreated himself as baby Krishna, son of the cowherd Nanda.

The twins, Sleep and Krishna, are a reminder of the male/ female aspect of Shiva. One can think of Sleep as the moon mother, the king as ego desires, the seven sacrificial embryos as levels of consciousness leading to the final goal of the eight-fold path of yoga, and baby Krishna is the young moon-god, the reborn. That is just one solution to the psychological dilemma offered by such myths. The important thing is how one personally relates the symbols – as an aid to Self-understanding.

The swastika, symbol of Aryanism, is derived from the four-armed gods and goddesses depicting the four moon aspects. Each month birth, death and resurrection can be observed in their continuous rotation in the sky. Try to relate this moon activity to the human's own mental seas, noticing the ebb and flow within the ocean of thought and instinct. Contemplate the moon of the mind – that part which reflects the light of the universal sun, Paramatma – and the constant movement shown by the revolving swastika or swirling crescents. Remember that nothing in creation is static. Ever-moving are mind, thought, desire . . . the revolving manifestations of karmically inherited tendencies and conditions. With illumination the wheel will take the human vehicle into higher realms, constellations of cosmic bliss.

One must act, one must move. But one has one's own choice of direction. To the extent that one connects with the Self within, one can create oneself anew. Krishna is called the womb of the universe . . . Guru of all who live within the three worlds. His mount is the bird Garuda, phoenix-like symbol of rebirth and enemy of the serpent of evil desires, of ignorance and duality, of negativity and anger. That gives a hint of the sort of work one must do in order to reach Krishna or cosmic consciousness.

It is said that all are female in relation to God. This may allude to the receptive attitude one assumes in contemplation and meditation. The confusion or switching of gender which ripples throughout mythology, in which gods and goddesses are often interchangeable, is a reflection of duality, opposite aspects of the same thing. Divinity sees no distinction between sexes. Indeed, when one realizes that one has lived many times in the physical garb of each gender, absence of real distinction takes on clearer meaning. In regard to Krishna, it is helpful to develop a nurturing, motherly reverence for one's own inner 'child', that tiny spark of godliness one wishes to encourage.

A beautiful story tells about Krishna's mother and her doubt. When the little cowherd children who played with Krishna told his mother that he had eaten dirt, he denied it, saying, "If you don't believe me, mother, see for yourself." As Yashoda opened her son's mouth she saw all of the universe there . . . space, time, earth, moon, mountains, water, every form of nature, the senses, the elements of consciousness, the gunas, wind, lightning . . . everything. She saw herself and the village she lived in with all its other inhabitants, people, cows, birds, trees and other creatures. Perhaps she was dreaming? She wondered if it was all an illusion of mind or if this being that was her son had done this to her. She bowed before her son, not able to grasp his nature with her mind or heart. She could not speak, could not fathom the depths of him, but she suddenly understood that ideas of 'my son . . . my husband . . . my wealth . . . I am this . . . I have that' were delusions. Essential truth illuminated her at this moment. Then she was captured once more in the web of maternal love through the power of the Infinite, who was embodied in that tiny child. She forgot her dream and held her beloved son, swept away in the floods of her own emotion. She had seen her limitations, beyond the human viewpoint, with the grace of the maker of dreams.

Two different psychological aspects are represented by the Krishna myths, one of Arjuna and the other of the gopis. Both eventually come to higher consciousness when negativity is abandoned. In the case of Arjuna, he could not reach the Ultimate through the analytical shortsightedness of his human mind; nor could he fight his battle with intellect. Meanwhile the gopis made the mistake of concentrating upon Krishna with desire. Until they evolved beyond body consciousness and ego, there was no chance for growth. Intellect and emotion gave way for the development of devotion once the distortions of mind and ego were surrendered. Krishna led Arjuna out of belief of doership and the gopis away from sensuality. It is important not to identify with the roles played in life. One is not the doer of acts. One is more than that – Atma.

To understand the gopi legends, we should think of the meaning of the cow symbol. The cows of the *Bhagavad Purana* were symbols of maternal love, although earlier myths used them as sacrificial animals, showing that the animal nature must be sacrificed by transmutation to a higher form. The cow was also a vehicle like Shiva's Nandi. Likewise, the human body is the vehicle given to assist growth on earth. Through yoga and discipline one can tune and perfect the body. It thus becomes one's servant – with the help of the Lord of Lords of Yoga.

As mentioned before, maternal love is the spirit of devotion needed to nurture the child of cosmic knowledge within. That is the part which is innocent, pure and wise beyond human understanding. The problem with the cowherd women was that they were tricked by their own fantasies into thinking that

Krishna was an object outside of themselves. They fell in love with illusion. Because of their failure to realize the essence of Krishna consciousness, they suffered the loss of the eleven-year-old child divinity. He was out of their grasp whenever they tried to project sensual fantasies upon him. To grow, the gopis had to mirror his childlike purity within themselves and forget their egoistic desires. The unfoldment of cosmic realization by the light of the full moon ceased as soon as the gopis' egos and personalities intervened. The flow of truth and understanding was interrupted and they were banished from the realm of cosmic bliss and enlightenment.

In order to reach Krishna, one must come to a state of utter humility, as shown by the story of the boy-god's pranks at the riverside where the gopis bathed. Having undergone spiritual disciplines for some time, the gopis sang praises to Krishna as they bathed in the river. Each had secret longings, however, that he would some day be hers alone. Krishna saw this as he and the other little cowherd boys, the gopas, watched. So he hid the girls' clothes. When he told them that they had violated their vows by consorting in this way with the god of the river, they were humiliated and mortified.

The clothes are layers of camouflage – mental conditioning and ego tendencies which must be removed. As the gopis leave the baptismal waters to bow before God their hands are raised above their heads, palms pressed together in reverence. All humans come from water, the symbol of birth, in the form of the watery environment of the mother's womb and also the primordial sea we left billions of years ago. Krishna stood in the tree of life, the symbol of stability and immortality, which stretches from its roots in the earth into the Infinite. The gopas stood nearby, giggling at the girls' predicament. The girls had to reveal their nakedness to overcome body consciousness and retrieve their clothes. It was a terrible test for them. They were told not to try to conceal themselves, but to bow to Krishna as they came near the tree. What is nakedness to God? Indeed, one must reveal one's true nature to oneself, removing previous conditioning and mental, emotional and physical obstructions in order to attain the purified cloak of spirituality.

Krishna said to the gopis, "The desire of those hearts who are placed in me do not lead to further desires, just as the seed corn that has been fried or boiled does not give rise to seed. You have achieved your aim . . . you are united with me through your devotion." He vowed to reveal cosmic consciousness to them, as long as they continued with their spiritual disciplines and practices. He used the circumstances at the riverside to abolish the gopis' self-concern, their feeling of separateness. They had been centred in selfish desires rather than Atma.

Considering that every being is a multitude, comprised of trillions of cells – an inner universe – it is foolish for one tiny cell to believe the Infinite could ever exclusively belong to it. The opposite is true. The Ultimate, the source of all that is and ever was and will be could never be possessed, contained or imprisoned within a limited space or form. That sort of imbalance is like a group of cells within a body which separate from the fold and start to increase themselves without maintaining the integrity of the whole, thus resulting in disease. Separateness is a corruption of spirituality. Krishna is the spoiler of such fantasies of ignorance, the liberator of minds.

After much urging from the gopis, who claimed that he gave more time to the gopas than to them, Krishna promised to reveal truth to them on the night of the full moon. By that time they had changed themselves by their sadhana and devotion, although their individual levels of development varied as in any group. Most had learned to feel Krishna within as they tended their herds, when doing yoga, as they cared for their husbands and children and throughout the performance of all duties. Every now and then they would come to a very high state . . . but it never lasted. As one who prays or meditates occasionally touches higher levels of consciousness, they reached out to growth and were anwered through Krishna that they would have their wish. However, when the long-awaited night arrived, the gopis felt apprehensive about what would happen. They went to Krishna with all sorts of questions regarding the mystery they were soon to witness . . . What should they do? They were afraid and tense. Krishna said, "Well, you wanted this, not I. It was you who said I was unfair. I do not care either way." So the gopis assured him they would go on with the meeting, though shocked by his decision on an hour when husbands, children and all other beings would be asleep.

Arjuna had had the same difficulty the gopis were having. In order to overcome ego, emotion, limitation of mind and body, social conditioning and samskaras, they had to break through blindness they had held to all their lives. Krishna wanted them to be free of all blocks and false ideas, wanted them to experience sattva, pure mind. One way or another, they all wanted to put conditions on their God, although they truly did crave enlightenment. Paramatma tried to make them understand that they – Jivatma – are nothing but Paramatma. Jivatma did not want to know this. That is the source of the conflict. Jivatma does not understand its pure form, but is bound by greed, lust, ego, emotion, ignorance, darkness and all sorts of negativity. The attributes of Paramatma, expressed in human terms, would be pure consciousness, brightness, beauty, grace, ultimate completeness and clarity. Paramatma wants Jivatma to merge, to become Paramatma. Jivatma is afraid of losing the separate ego . . . it wants . . . it does not want . . . it cannot decide. When surrounded by negative influences, the human does not respond to spiritual inspiration; when influenced by positive stimuli, it longs for liberation. In order to attain Paramatma, Jivatma must realize the traps of such subtle tendencies – the gunas – and learn to proceed courageously to the higher state of being. Thus there are some aspects left which threaten to pull the gopi-disciples back down to the animal level illustrated by their nearness to the horses, cows and goats, the four-footed beings they tend. They are not certain nor stable yet. Although they had been able to relax in their new-found serenity while doing their work, they were hesitant and shaky as the great night arrived. Still, they went to the forest at midnight, the time of sleep and dreams, accompanied by their animals, who waited in the groves of trees surrounding the wonderful clearing where the event would occur.

The gopis had heard the clarion call which had awakened

them from sleep. Like a herd of wild horses they had run to meet their fate beneath a giant, luminous full moon which spread its glorious rays throughout the forests, exciting the trees, plants, insects and all other animals who anticipated the play of cosmic consciousness which would unfold. Silently they waited and watched. All of the elements of nature were prepared. The wind was a gentle breeze, the clouds placed themselves decoratively in the dark sky and the air was sweet and fragrant. Krishna sat on a rock, as if on a throne, and the gopis encircled him. Then he told them something they did not expect. "You have no sense of duty or responsibility that you leave your husbands and children and come to meet a man in the forest at night. Is that rightness of mind or purity of intention? Go back now, all of you. It is not right for you to be here." There was complete silence, as all were petrified and shocked. "Aha! Now he shows his true nature. What a crafty Krishna this is, who has tricked us once more." They were terribly upset, whispering and murmuring to each other. But they did not leave. That was the last test. Krishna could see they were determined to go on, no matter the outcome. They were committed to growth and had overcome their sense of physical consciousness. They were no longer relating on the human level, and there was nothing wrong in their hearts.

The great cosmic play – the Krishna Lila – commenced with music, dance and song of infinite beauty. It lasted not just one hour or night, but millions of nights. The moon would not dare to cease shining while Krishna was unfolding his profound play of enlightenment. It shone for millions of nights, and the humans who slept were unaware of the length of time which passed. As the experience continued, each gopi became deluded that Krishna was relating to her alone. The human ego and illusion of duality seeped into the gopis' collective consciousness, and the cosmic unfoldment stopped . . . the Lord of Dreams vanished from their midst . . . They awakened from the beautiful reverie of blissful truth and landed back on the earthly plane. It was like sleep, they had surrendered their consciousness to the dreamworld, where the bodily functions were less encumbered and the ego was replaced by another part of the being which could receive more profound experience than in the waking state. But as soon as their separate identities and selfish desires entered the picture, the dream ended. They were jolted awake, banished from the bliss of a moment before.

The gopis stood alone under the trees, crying and regretting, for they knew exactly what they had done. How could such base instincts have come to mind to ruin their chance of fulfilment? They asked the trees, the animals and all the other creatures where Krishna had gone; then noticed that one of them, the most evolved, had disappeared with Krishna. "Look, again he has taken Radha with him . . . why not me?" They were very upset. But wherever a slight bit of ego exists, the possibility of returning to the lower level also remains. The gopis were relieved when Radha rejoined them. Although more developed spiritually than the rest, she also became the victim of her ego; when she found herself alone with God, she thought she was special. Determined to uplift themselves, and more aware than ever of their downfall, the gopis vowed to find Krishna consciousness again. Eventually they achieved that aim. As accounted in the Mahabharata, they participated in the cosmic play and merged into the Infinite. After that enlightenment, the gopis never met Krishna in physical form. When they were brought to such a high level of awareness, being always with Krishna, the body did not matter.

That beloved, blissful consciousness which is one's other half – Paramatma – is already within, waiting to be revealed. That is the divine unity all creatures crave and seek unconsciously. That is the possessor of siddhis (special powers), the master, the knower of truth and cosmic totality. To come closer to that revelation, one must purify thought, speech and action, consecrating everything one does to higher growth, to the Divine: Krishna, Shiva, Christ . . . whichever manifestation represents that Ultimate to one's mind. The control of prana (life force), through hatha yoga and pranayama can be very helpful, but the most important thing is to control the mind. Prana sustains and nourishes – one breathes in cosmic energy and exhales toxins and poisons accumulated from metabolic processes and negative thought. Anything one touches, sees or hears becomes part of body and mind. Since one is the sum total of everything contacted and received, one manifests according to one's imagination and choice. Thought and energy are created from those things one assimilates in one's environment and one becomes subject to one's own creation. That can be a frightening thought. What is outside becomes inside. Every act is important.

One can do things unconsciously, out of habit, which then affects thought, awareness and subsequent action. It can be a vicious system of self-destructive behaviour repeating itself in cycles. The body is a vehicle, a tool, to be used, or misused. It is a builder of karma and an energy re-cycling machine. The aim of yoga is unity and understanding of body, mind and life itself. Balance is the essence. Not one thing is more important than anything else; the integrity of the whole must be sought. Through management of life-force and the manifestation of one's higher Self within the consciousness one can achieve contentment, completeness and harmony, get rid of conditioning, mental pollution, habits and biases of thought which stand in the way. Let the experience of life be new, fresh. Exhale slowly and completely . . . inhale deeply and fully. Feel the moon as part of the mind, reflecting the omniscient sun of the Source . . . filling you with light and expanding the consciousness of Self. Sense the Universal Spirit sending its rays of truth into your awareness as you drift off into the healing arms of Sleep, Krishna's sister. All the beauty of the universe can be reflecting in that glowing orb of mind. The Christian religion holds the same symbolism, a little child will lead you. That child is one's own perfect, pure childlikeness. That is the devotion and innocent humility that emerges when mind is uplifted like a full beaming moon held in the infinite sea of consciousness. That is the source of ambrosia, soma, immortality. It is the light that illumines the darkness of unconsciousness. It is the banner of evolution. Breathe once more . . . "SO" . . . exhale . . . "HAM" . . . "I AM THAT!"

7
Poorna Yoga

Fain would I stretch me by the highway side
To thaw and trickle with the melting snow
That mingled, soul and body, with the tide
I too may through the pores of nature flow.

THOREAU

Thousands of years ago, in the Age of Truth, the scientific system of yoga was created by highly evolved humanists and sages who knew that a darker time would come when humankind would hunger for such guidance. In the caves of the Himalayas, amidst the forests and rivers of that ancient land, those profound minds wove the fabric of the Vedas. Thus the pattern for total unfolding of human potential – Poona Yoga – was clarified. In Sanskrit poorna (pūrná) means complete, whole, total. Yoga implies unity, integrity, balance and attunement to nature. It is a method of growth based on physical fitness, mental profoundness and Self-realization. If the individual grows, all of life grows. Yoga is not a religion, a political movement or a dogma; it is a way of bringing harmony within diversity. It respects all cultures, creeds and nations, and it nurtures the higher instincts of humanity; compassion, co-operation and peace.

It is not difficult to see the place of yoga in modern life. The Vedic scholars did indeed have great foresight in devising a blueprint for evolution. Kali Yuga, the age in which we now find ourselves, is complicated and confusing. It is the age of iron, space age, computer age, machine age. Our so-called progressive developments have brought us to the brink of war and destruction. We are addicted to technology. So much emphasis is placed on the many gadgets we like to play with,

99

and so little energy is spent on the more important aspects of our lives. How far have we really advanced? Eighty percent of the world's population does not have the technological advantage which the remaining twenty percent enjoys. If, as many believe, the world is at the edge of an energy disaster, it is not the eighty percent who will suffer (they will not miss what they never had), but it is the twenty percent who will be miserable. So much of what we call civilization is built upon illusion. It may crumble at any time leaving us wondering what happened and never seeing what might have been done to stop the negative progression.

The introduction of yoga into everyday life is more essential now than ever. By yoga many problems can be overcome; lack of memory, confusion, distorted personality, wrong qualities emphasized in life, human disunity, physical and mental imbalances such as depression and suicide. It engenders peaceful coexistence and co-operation and supports the natural mind which reveals itself once the encumbrances of mental conditioning, karmically inherited tendencies and illusions are lifted. It is a cleansing process. To deny yoga is to deny moon, sun, oceans, space, all aspects of nature. Yoga is universal. It is a means of research, exploration and expansion on many levels. Life itself is yoga. Indeed yoga is a far-reaching term and a vast subject. It is like a huge, majestic tree that stands for expansion of heart, mind and Self. Rooted in nature it branches out into innumerable realms of creativity, blossoming with bliss and the fulfilment of all human potential.

It is quite appropriate for humans to feel harmony with nature, especially when seeking higher, natural growth. Nature is our inspiration and our mother. Throughout the ages sadhakas and sages dedicated their lives to living in harmony with the natural forces within themselves and in their environment. In Vedic times some trees were revered as if they were High Beings. They were appreciated for their uplifting influence, and higher teaching was often given in their midst. It is a scientifically proven fact that trees create a change in the atmosphere (known as negative ionization) which affects the brainwave pattern of humans causing the alpha state, which one experiences in the first stages of meditation. It is easy to understand how wise men like Rabindranath Tagore, having no 'institute' as such, began teaching in the openness of nature where there were no walls to limit growth nor boundaries to enclose the imagination. Dance, music, writing, philosophy . . . all went on under trees. Swami Sivananda Sarasvati, once a successful surgeon of South India, renounced the world and went to the Himalayas to undergo spiritual disciplines, contemplation and meditation on the banks of the Ganges. After that he started a camp with a few disciples in the Himalayan forests. Of course, the story of Buddha and his Bodhi Tree is well known. Four walls may protect you, but they also hold you in. The symbol of the tree, with its strength and expansion, also applies to the way one approaches learning. One must be receptive, open, without clinging to conditions of mind (mental walls), without preventing one's own expansion by forgetting one's roots (one's nature).

> The body is the first and obvious reality.
> The mind is the relative reality.
> The Self is the Ultimate Reality.

One may not experience the second and third reality, but all humans are involved with the first. It is the hard reality of us. This body is a vehicle to carry us onward into experience of the other realities. But in order to reach the final destination, one must be fit and sound. The body cannot be ignored by the individual or by society. In the system of yoga the body is important to begin with. We never start at the end in any teaching. If instant samadhi were attainable, this might be possible. The path is long and hard, and those who wish to travel it must develop extreme strength and endurance, physically and otherwise. Many do not realize that the physical body is designed and intended to live normally 150 years. That is without being a High Yogi, who may extend that time enormously. Living in this sense means remaining healthy, sound and fit until age 150. It seems that one thing humankind has mastered is the ability to shorten its own lifespan. Most people do not live in health beyond 50, and extension of life is often an extension of suffering rather than health. In some of the lesser developed nations the average lifespan is 35 years.

Some people think, "What will I do all that time? Who wants to live that long? It would be so boring." Today it is normal for people to retire at 55 or 60 years. They are often bored, depressed and become unfit because they have been told indirectly that they are no longer useful to society. People who do have time do not seem to know what to do with it, and those who have no time are busy doing nothing.

The question is how to keep this body in good working order for its full lifespan and also how to get it to carry one into realms of increased creativity and fulfilment. Boredom evaporates once one knows how to live, create and proceed to the goal of life. Firstly, to live 150 years one must de-programme oneself out of negativity. However one is programmed, the mind, senses and body function accordingly. The brain, that incredibly complex computer, does its work by following the data it has been fed. If one plants a tree of thorns one cannot expect it to bear sweet fruit. The brain is made up of billions of cells or circuits, tiny entities working unitedly and independently to serve one's every whim and desire. They respond to each thought one creates, both fear and fancy. Whatever is programmed will be unfolded.

One should analyze one's day; what one has thought, said, done, eaten, imagined. It is a reasonable estimate that eighty or ninety percent of one's thought, action and performance has been negatively dominated. A small percentage has been positive, and for that one is proud. Assessing this estimate, can one truly expect body and mind to be healthy, fit and sound? If most of one's energy is used to promote unhealthy vibration, what is the result? One does not have to be a computer expert to figure it out. One's job is to start this moment to de-programme oneself. Yoga can be the tool. Hatha yoga is a complete system of physical maintenance. Meditation creates positive vibration throughout the entire being, and contemplation is the most effective method of psychology known to this earth. By simply letting one's thoughts appear, without getting involved with them, without being affected but merely observing, one enables the energy held by the thoughts to dissipate and release its charge of negativity. In this way one removes the faulty mental conditioning one has retained during one's lifetime, that very illusion which programmes one to expect less from life than one deserves. The whole attitude and approach that most people have is damaging to life, both physically and mentally. It does no good to seek help from this or that agency outside oneself. Introspection is the master tool. If the computer's programming is not in order, the body will not be in order. And if the body is not in proper order, nothing else in life will work. A headache will prevent one from appreciating all the riches of the world. Gold, diamonds and all the ornaments of the Maharajas will hardly please one without health.

Once one understands the politics and technique of the body things begin to come without the slightest effort. One learns to manage energy in the way that nature intended and one functions within the flow of a vibratory stream that carries one along with ease. The body then is no longer a hindrance, full of aches and pains, but a proper vehicle for further growth. Actually, it is a masterpiece of cosmic creation. It represents the entire cosmos in miniature form. Just think: each person represents the totality and completeness of the Ultimate. The body is more than flesh and blood, and every individual has a responsibility to care for that which is given to be used (not abused) in the quest for Truth. It is something unique and profound. It is a symbol, as are all manifestations on the material plane. It is a medium for expression of something beyond this earthly plane. We must try to understand, study and care for this instrument. Once we see the relationship between body and mind clearly, we can start to move towards growth beyond body and mind. This can be accomplished through the concentrated practice of hatha yoga. It is not something that is learned only from books; it must be applied to living.

Yogis do not know disease. Their bodies are taught to enjoy and expect health as a normal fact of life. Everything they need they have. If left to its own devices the body will cure itself. The cure is within. By using chemicals the body decays; it crumbles and eventually breaks down from the accumulated deposits in its various pathways and circuits. It becomes clogged and overworked by the obstructions of sediment it was never made to handle. Once one sets the body right on the basis of Yoga, there will be no reason for disease to manifest. One makes oneself complete, free.

Body and mind will follow one's dictates as long as one respects nature. One should not subject oneself to objects; one is above them. There is no yoga without health and no health without yoga. One must be strong to experience bliss and enlightenment. Physical exercises, breath control, sense control, meditation, relaxation and calm must be introduced into everyday life. This foundation must first be formed. With practice one will eventually be able to enter into more profound dimensions of yogic experience.

Many people have difficulty when they begin to meditate. They attempt to 'conquer' meditation, as if it were the enemy. That will never work. One must drift naturally into the meditative state. It may help to be among the calming greenery of plants and trees or near the ocean. Nature has a way of taking us more deeply into ourselves when we give her the chance. Without forcing, try to dive into the deep ocean within. Relax and let that part which is neither body nor mind emerge. Let the body become radiant with the energy of its own magnetic field, surrounded and filled with cosmic light. That very energy is prevalent everywhere in the universe. One is made of the essence of stars and galaxies. Relax more and more; feel that the heart and mind are relaxing, that stress is evaporating and all thoughts are simply floating by like clouds suspended in a clear sky. Let thoughts and outside disturbances go without much notice. The mind rests in silence. The heart is nourished and each power circuit, each vertebra, begins to vibrate with energy. Feel that energy is circulating from the base of the spine to the top of the head . . . continuously flowing . . . unobstructed and free. Feel well, healthy and sustained by cosmic energy which supports all life – every element, every aspect of creation.

One may wish to concentrate on the chakras, wheels of energy situated at various points along the spine. There are seven and they correspond to levels of consciousness. When the circuits are free-flowing, physical as well as mental energies are transmuted. But when the energy flow is blocked, distortion and illusion result. Enlightenment is the end-product of liberation from the barriers we place upon ourselves. The important thing is to remove all the blocks that stand in the way.

The first chakra, Muladhara (the root chakra), is located at the base of the spine. Here lies the source of physical strength and stability. Profound energy transmutes into a powerful creative source. The second chakra is Svadhisthana, located in the lower abdomen; it represents an expansive growth urge. While the first centre tends to give the feeling of survival instinct, the second is an urge to maintain and preserve. Greed, envy and lust result when one is stuck at this point. The third chakra, Manipura, is the centre of ego, emotion and the sense of self-assertion, the power urge. The fourth is called Anahata, the heart chakra, home of love, compassion, humanitarianism and burgeoning wisdom. The fifth chakra, Visuddha, is located in the throat area. Knowledge of a higher sort, integrating internal and external realities, manifests here. One who has reached this stage of consciousness hears the sound of silence (Nadam) and sees far beyond the illusions which blind most humans. Ajna chakra, the sixth centre, is associated with wisdom and powers such as clairvoyance and perfect intuition. Detachment, asceticism, complete calm and stability of mind result at this level of vibration. The seventh chakra is Sahasrara, or crown chakra. This is the highest, the thousand-petalled lotus – seat of creativity, peace and bliss. It is the centre of ultimate unity and enlightenment. These centres can be experienced in meditation by visualizing the qualities as one breathes slowly, sending energy into each centre and beyond into the next. It is best not to concentrate on a singular chakra but to send energy through, focusing the breath upward from the base of the spine to the top of the head

. . . free-flowing. The idea is to open up the circuits, not to get stuck at any one point along the way. Maintain the thought that everything one needs one has within. One can help oneself remove all the blocks. After all, it is the individual who put them there in the first place. Visualize energy flowing through . . . feel Infinity manifesting within.

It may be helpful to repeat the following sounds as one imagines energy coursing through the chakras, one by one:

> 1st chakra . . . SRING
> 2nd chakra . . . HRING
> 3rd chakra . . . KLING
> 4th chakra . . . BHRING
> 5th chakra . . . LRING
> 6th chakra . . . SOHAM
> 7th chakra . . . PURNAM

Repeat each sound at least seven times while concentrating on the corresponding centre. The effect of these mantras is to activate and purify certain nerves and to remove any blockage in the circuitry which runs along the spine to the brain. Remember to breathe in energy and to exhale poisons and negativity; and always remain relaxed. After meditating, slowly rotate the head first in one direction and then in the opposite direction. (This is good to do at any time in the day when one feels under stress.)

This is a beautiful mantra for greeting the sun:

> OM NAMO SURYAYA
> OM NAMO BHASKRAYA
> OM NAMO DIVAYA
> OM NAMO TEJAYA
> OM MANO PRKASHAYA

Meaning:

1st line: I recognize the sun within me; it is the cause, the dweller of my life. On that basis life functions. This energy is the energy that flows through me.

2nd line: Its sustenance is sparkling into every cell of my body, vital energy spreading throughout, new rays incessantly beaming into me.

3rd line: This is my source of nourishment; it creates new life in me.

4th line: This promotes brightness and vitality in me.
5th line: It enlightens me, fills me with knowledge, dissolves darkness. I invoke the sun, source of my life, and I place you, sun, in my body . . . so that it may function fully . . . to the last cell.

A mantra is not a prayer nor a religious hymn but a technique by which one can increase one's own energy. It is a method of psychosomatic healing. Whether or not one understands the Sanskrit terms is not so important; the sounds will still have the desired effect. There is an entire form of yoga based upon sound therapy – mantra yoga. Certain 'seed' syllables have within them the power to affect the nerves and glands. 'Soham' is one very significant mantra, a "seed" that one can plant deep within the psyche by repetition; the fruit it engenders will assist growth far beyond its five letters. Sound is vibration, and that is such a powerful thing it can create or destroy. It can kill or it can cure in the form of laser beams and as ultra-sound.

Closely related to mantra yoga are several other schools of yoga which also use sound to change body chemistry and uplift the mental faculties. Laya yoga involves tone and melody. Gita or sangita yoga has to do with song and creating music with various instruments, not only the well-known classical string and wind instruments but also through the use of stones, spoons and any implement the mind can create. The variety, colourfulness and beauty of music made in these ways is astounding. Music and yoga are linked. In ashrams it is sometimes the practice to begin meditation early in the morning with the performance of music. Thus an atmosphere is created which leads to deeper states of experience. Then physical yoga takes one into another dimension. Each pore vibrates and radiates peaceful energy as, one by one, various forms of practice take one further and further. Concentration then leads to contemplation which moves one into meditation until, at last, one proceeds into samadhi, the highest state of consciousness. Music is definitely an important tool. One of the highest practices is Nada Brahman yoga. There is one Nada yogi now in America who has mystified scientists with the music he creates mentally. He closes the nine gates,* cuts off the outside world, and with the frequency of his brain waves he composes exquisite patterns of tone which can be measured by use of very sensitive scientific instruments. Fascinating music has been recorded from his brain waves. Think how Beethoven composed music when he was unable to hear. Deafness in the clinical sense is certainly not the total silence one would assume. Music, like colour, is made of vibrating waves of energy.

Silence speaks loudly indeed when inner creativity begins to unfold. One reaches a state in music as in meditation where nothing exists, not even oneself. Totality can thus be achieved – oneness with everything. One becomes energy, sound, light, music. Nothing is separate; one is the cosmos, the absolute, bliss. Music knows no barriers of caste, creed, race, religion or philosophy. It belongs to no ideology. It is a language beyond words which needs no translation. It is yoga. Different pieces of music (ragas) can be performed for nearly every time of day to assist meditation. Once one has come to the stage of hearing the sound of silence, the external forms cease to enthral. It should be mentioned that the music being discussed is not used to inflate the senses but to help growth.

Mere sentiment is unprofitable in the quest for higher knowledge, it is wasted energy. And so much noise that calls itself music these days is hardly more than traffic commotion in terms of aesthetics. This negative aspect of consciousness spilling into the area of music is just another symptom of our society's distortion. For instance, in recent incidents people have trampled on and even killed one another while 'enjoying' rock concerts. This is the opposite side of where one wants to go, musically and otherwise. The song of Krishna in the battlefield of the *Bhagavad Gita* says:

Life itself is a battle.
To fight life one must be brave.
Those who are brave enough to fight with themselves –
They can fight the entire world.

* The nine openings of the physical body.

He is singing about the fight against ignorance, ego and negativity within oneself. He is not talking about stampeding for electronically induced music that makes people mad. He is not saying we should all go out and fight wars over this or that ideology. The battle he refers to is not sport nor entertainment but the struggle for life itself. It is a creative battle, not one of destruction. It is the battle of yoga as taught by the Lord of Lords of yoga Himself – Krishna. It is interesting to note that He was also the master musician so often pictured playing His flute.

In the sixteenth century there lived in India the great Mogul Emperor Akbar. He loved the arts and sciences and promoted both as no Mogul ruler before or since. He would gather the best musicians to perform in his court. Some were so adept that they could create the sensation of heat, so much so that the audience would perspire. When the music stopped, the heat which at times reached the point of burning also ceased. This classical music of India was so refined and powerful that it affected the listeners to their very last cell. On hot days, coolness could be created to soothe them. People would weep, laugh and experience all manner of emotional sensation through its masterful use of vibration. When a musician entered the court of Akbar, he was asked not what kind of music he performed, but rather what quality was his speciality. They could create both subtle and gross effects. One who came to Akbar's attention claimed he could make such profound music that all the animals in the land would gather around. The Emperor did not believe this but told the man he would be given a great title if he could indeed accomplish that. So the performance was arranged. After the musician had played for fifteen or twenty minutes, all the animals in the area started to congregate, including the insects.

At the beginning of creation the great Eternal Being Shiva performed the Tandava – the great cosmic dance – upon Mt Kailasa. This image of the dancing Shiva became famous around the world in sculptured masterpieces, some of which are priceless. As He danced in a circle of fire, Shiva played a drum, beating it fourteen times to form the first alphabet of the universe. From this alphabet the first language, Brahmi, evolved, the ancestor of Sanskrit. Brahmi was the mother of all languages of the world and the tongue of highly evolved beings such as Dhanavantri, author of the *Ayurveda* (the oldest treatise of health maintenance), and other Great Ones who gave their knowledge to humanity. The literal meaning of the word Sanskrit is 'one who is cultured, well-mannered, behaved; one who has orderliness and system to his actions'. Sanskrit is itself a perfect system of communication, for it has no exceptions to its grammatical rules. By knowing Sanskrit one can understand and create spontaneous expressions according to time and need. Whatever new form is created will be totally understood by others. There is no other language which facilitates communication in this way. It was in this tongue that the great medical, philosophical and musical treatises, the Vedas, were given by those illuminated sages who lived simply but profoundly in the caves and forests of the Himalayas while the rest of the world struggled in primitive darkness, as it does again today.

India can claim something no other country can. In its classic time it was accepted that no matter what one did, whether it was music, dance, painting, pottery, sculpture, etc., it was not for the purpose of material reward but as a means to advance one's higher growth. It was accepted that through art one grew and through higher growth art flourished. Those who taught music or dance were called gurus. The idea of yogic growth and its application to modern life is similar. The main focus of one's life must be the attainment of enlightenment through one's activities on earth. If money, fame and power come, they are by-products. Feel joy for whatever work needs to be done; not grumbling because one has to do it and hates it. It is wonderful when one likes one's work, but if the work is something not particularly enjoyable one should use it as spiritual practice and discipline; as sadhana and tapasya. Thereby one grows through experience.

The literal meaning of tapas is 'to burn it'. It is the process in which iron is put into fire so that when it is very hot it can be taken out and moulded, beaten into its final shape as a tool or instrument. To the seeker who is prepared to go through this process in order to become evolved, the disciplines involved may seem quite difficult at times. They are not; it only seems a painful and complex process because of conditions of mind. Sadhana constitutes the various methods by which fulfilment is attained, though it is less severe than tapasya. The latter appears to be rougher, but to those who have gone through all that, there is no severity. They are aware of relativity. It is always possible that one person's pleasure is another's pain, and vice versa. It depends on the motivation and depth of understanding. The best attitude is to transmute everything into positivity. No matter what one faces in life, take it as a lesson, a test, a challenge and an opportunity to grow. Then grow one will.

A High Being was busy planting rice. When a man came and asked him how to get enlightenment, the wise one answered, "It is not difficult, it is just like planting rice. You take the plant from here and put it there, in the other field." The essence is transformation. One removes oneself from the self-created entanglements and conditions and puts oneself in a totally new place, outside the walls one had built before. Thinking, behaviour and mental programming must change. Once emptied of all the psychological formations one has carried around as 'personality' all these years one begins to get new insight. A vessel can only be filled once it is empty. Perception changes as consciousness grows. If one looks at the view of earth from space, humans look insignificant. This tiny planet can fit into Jupiter one thousand times. Yet we are the troublemakers of the universe. Basing justice upon ego, greed and false ideas of power, cosmic law is ignored.

If one looks at the structure of one cell's nucleus, one will see a moonscape with mountainous areas, valleys and craters. Is all of this illusion, some trick of vision, an optical blur – or is it reality? It is a simple truth that perception changes with the variance of angle. This is the relative reality of the mind, which was mentioned earlier (the second reality). Even science supports this fact. Yet science is limited in comprehending the complex network of nature's illusion. The reality of energy, the Unlimited, that which no mind can comprehend, is larger than the measure which seeks to confine it. The lower laws of physics will destroy those who centre their lives upon them. One must go further to find higher laws; all else is relative, limited.

In modern times one very wealthy man went to a sage in India hoping to be guided, with the wise one's help, to realization of higher Truth.

"Please. Tell me the way to attain That."

"All right. Take the brush and sweep the ground."

"But . . . ."

"Not 'but' and no 'if'. You have come here to attain the Highest and I tell you to sweep the ground."

So he takes the brush and begins to sweep, and when he has finished he returns to tell the wise man.

"I have completed, now you tell me."

"Take that bowl, go to the village and bring food back with you."

"But how can I . . . ."

"Not 'but' and no 'if' . . . I tell you to go there."

So he goes to the village where he is unknown and he starts to beg for food. The people there do not like what they see – a strong, well-built man with good appearance. What need has he to beg food? At one house the lady householder comes out and begins to shout at him, "You have a strong body, can't you use it to work? Why do you beg for food? You should be ashamed of yourself." The man at last cannot bear the verbal abuse he encounters from house to house and returns to the wise man without food. The guru disqualifies him from further teaching and sends him home. But he becomes restless, unable to sleep, confused, and cannot comprehend the strange behaviour of this guru. He does not understand the meaning of sweeping the floor or going to the village to beg food. "I could give him tons of food or employ a hundred servants to sweep his floor. Why does he want me to do that?" The link between all that and enlightenment totally escapes him. He is not one to give up, though, and he returns the next day to visit the wise man.

"I am here again. I will do whatever you ask."

"Good. Take that bowl, go to another village and bring back food. Not the same village, where they may have compassion for you. Go to another place."

At the second village he is again insulted and cursed, but somehow he manages to get food. To his amazement, when he offers the food to the guru he is told:

"Give it to the birds and go back to your home.

You are disqualified."

At home he finds no rest. He thinks, "I got the food. I was forced to endure curses and abuse. Still he does not accept me. What does he want? I can get everything in the world; I have millions of dollars, heaps of gold, silver, diamonds, power, and still I cannot get what I want." After some time he returns to the guru. He is sent to get food from a third village. He goes and this time is received well. The people praise him, offer him anything he wants. That is it. Finally someone gives him the respect he deserves. Enlightenment must be close at hand. But once more he is disqualified. What a strange guru. He cannot be pleased either way. Not wanting to give it all up, the man goes to a fourth village, is met with curses and abuse, but he listens patiently, remains undisturbed. At the next house he is met with praise and flattery. Again he feels nothing. He thinks all of that unimportant. Finally, when he returns, the guru eats the food. He is qualified for further teaching.

"Can you please explain why I had to go through all that?"

"Yes. When you first came back without food, having been humiliated by the people, what did you feel, why did you come back?"

"I thought that I can afford to feed thousands of people, I have tons of food, and what right does this woman have to tell me off; I, who am . . . ."

"You see, that is the point."

"Why did you not accept the food I brought after being praised?"

"Again you felt 'I am this . . . I am that'. Until now you had been identifying yourself with things, thoughts, ideas which are not true. It hurt your ego when you were told off.

It pleased your ego when you were praised. You reacted. The false identity that you are mind, you are body, you are a rich man, etc., disqualified you. Finally you came to see that praises and insults do not matter . . . they are of no concern to one who knows what one really is."

Discipline of body, mind, emotions and senses is essential to a well-integrated life, and it is certainly necessary on the yogic path. One creates anxiety, fear and stress through lack of self-control. Yoga seeks to correct this imbalance through various processes devised at the time of the Vedas. That they are more applicable to life now than ever shows the depth of wisdom and knowledge in the great sages who created them. Patanjali's Eightfold Path of Yoga prescribes restriction, observation, asanas (physical exercises), pranayama (control of life force through breathing techniques), pratyahara (control of senses), dharana (contemplation), dhyana (meditation), leading to the final state samadhi (highest, cosmic consciousness or supraconsciousness). People sometimes ask "Why does a yogi or yogini have to observe so many rules? Are they not bound by all that restriction?" Certainly the yogi and yogini do not want any kind of imprisonment, but they see the need for order in life. There is nothing in the world more binding than ignorance. One is bound by emotional instability, distorted ego, senses that rule. In order to gain complete control over body, mind and ego one must take hold firmly of the reins, never letting these wild horses run away from their master. First one must realize who the master is – Atma, one's higher Self. That is the third reality mentioned earlier, the Ultimate Reality. If that is one's goal, one is willing to go through any hardship to attain it. The disciplines one integrates into one's life voluntarily will not cause resentment or negativity. Only the strongest of will can enter into that path.

People may use the excuse that they have no will power, forgetting that will-power is like all other aspects of body and mind in the sense that the more it is exercised the more it develops. Once it has been strengthened it becomes a force which flows effortlessly, of its own accord. Many yogic practices are focused upon enhancement of will. In India one may see a sadhu staring all day at the sun or standing for days in a frigid river. There are those who stand for years and others who will not speak for a decade. Such extremes are not for everyone, of course, but are illustrations that determination must be so strong that nothing can dissuade one from the search for Truth. Yoga implies balance in everything. Once the senses are regularized they will not rule. Once the mind is relaxed it will not prevent clear thinking. Once the body is purified through asanas and dietary discretion the senses will also be cleansed. Once the will is focused upon the goal the emotions will cease to confuse. All these aspects work in unity; each affects the others. One is not made up of bits and pieces. One is a totality.

The fourth fold of the Patanjali system of Yoga is the management of life energy – pranayama. It involves at least five hundred breathing techniques, some of which specialize in building the heart and lungs to capacity so these organs will know no exhaustion. By this practice yogis are able to increase the amount of oxygen they take in, and they can also manage to exist quite efficiently and energetically with whatever limited oxygen the atmosphere affords. In this way they can live in areas where air is a rarity, such as Himalayan summits, twenty or twenty-two thousand feet above sea level. With this amount of control they are also able to prolong their lives. This is the control regulation and integration of prana, the energy force by which life is sustained. It is known as cosmic energy, life-source, the breath of life. It is one's own energy and the energy of one's environment. To develop breathing faculties, begin by slow, even, deep breathing, breath retention exercises, and alternate nostril breathing. As you inhale, think that you are taking in healing energy – you are being cleansed and revitalized. As you exhale, imagine yourself expelling all the poisons and waste products of metabolism – even negative thoughts and ideas that block you are leaving, not just emptying from your lungs, but from every pore.

Prana is the main aspect of life force; it is the fuel of the body. There are also four lesser pranas: apana, udana, vyana and samana. They concern different functions of the body such as digestion, perspiration and elimination. Yogis have such control of this system that they can close all the bodily entrances and generate prana from within themselves, remaining without 'breath' for long periods. One of the mudras of higher yoga is called Kechari Mudra and involves use of the tongue to block the flow of air into the nose and throat. In the first place the yogi must sever or stretch a segment of the underside of the tongue to achieve this. Then he must also have perfected his ability to create prana from within or his heart will not continue to work. Clearly fear is one of the first things to be controlled on the yogic paths. It is not for the squeamish. By prana control yogis are able to clean practically every organ; thus the body can be purified. The digestive capacity can be increased so much that one is able to digest iron, mercury, gold and other heavy metals. These substances are purified within the body and the energy is extracted from them. This helps one to overcome extremes of climate, pain, illness, etc., and promotes the acquisition of supra-normal powers, mental as well as physical. Many accomplishments of yogis absolutely mystify modern science. It is a fact that where so-called modern science ends the science of yoga begins. This science is more subtle; it does not always comply with accepted scientific limitations.

It has been observed that methods which are in any way uncommon or unusual can cause widespread controversy and confusion. The unconventional, the unfamiliar is often considered exciting and shocking. It is sad that instead of examining and analyzing mindfully, the human being reacts by rejecting what it has not even tried to understand. Science as it is known today is not all, one has to break the conditioning of mind and media to widen one's horizon.

Various industrial sectors try to convince people that people need them or their product for health and benefit. On the contrary, it is they who need the people's money for their own financial health and benefit.

To break through the conditioning of the advertising media, a discriminating mind is necessary. Look how romantic cigarettes are made to appear. We would assume that cigarettes have the ability to make us sensuous, slender and successful, if we believed those powerful advertising slogans.

Please understand that the idea is not to revolt against anything; yoga is not a violent system. One must learn to think for oneself.

As yoga practice proceeds one becomes more sensitive to one's needs. One develops discrimination, physically as well as mentally. Without thinking one begins to sense what will promote health and what will destroy it. Fasting a day or two, drinking only lemon juice in pure water, may help cleanse the system of chemicals consumed in food or water. It is also a good exercise of will-power and tends to quiet the mind, especially if combined with the observance of total silence. It is best to eat foods that are fresh and, if possible, raw. Many important elements are destroyed in the cooking process. Enzymes, for instance, are needed for innumerable biological processes within the body but they have no chance to survive when exposed to heat. Certain foods are best avoided: meat and highly processed, devitalized products can create infection and contamination of the blood. Decide to eat only those foods which increase vitality – live and natural foods.

In terms of restrictions, Patanjali taught that one should not harm others, should not hurt any creature, should not steal, lie or take away the rights of another. One also should not be afraid, should not allow oneself to be victimized, should not turn away from the fight against injustice and negativity when one is faced with that. If you see someone hurting someone else, you have an obligation to try to stop that. If someone is in pain or trouble and you can aid in some way, do it. If people can benefit from what you know, give them your knowledge. Do not interfere in the lives of others to assert yourself. Your main job is to observe yourself, purify your intentions and grow through whatever situations your karma produces. By acting, thinking and speaking rightly, you create good karma to counteract any bad karma you have. That is karma yoga, the path of action. It concerns the way in which you deal with situations that confront you, with your ability to remain unaffected and detached. This does not mean you are passive;

on the contrary, you perform as perfectly as possible every activity life requires. But your focus is neither on the fruits of action nor on the idea that you are the performer of action. You are not the doer. Things get done, but you identify only with the Ultimate. In this way every aspect of your 'external' life becomes sadhana (spiritual practice). You come to see the Ultimate Reality in everything. You either accept that you are part of everything, or that you are part of nothing, that you are beyond. Everything is in you and you are in everything, for all are aspects of the One. This yoga can make one quite humble. The idea is service.

When one devotes one's life to serving a guru, that is called seva. It is active work motivated by devotion (bhakti). Any act done selflessly is seva.

In bhakti emotions are chanelled into creative rather than destructive activities. Prayer, devotional songs and meditation focused upon the guru – Buddha, Krishna, Christ, or living teacher – become instrumental in transmuting the powerful energies of emotion into higher levels of expression. It is true that whatever one sets one's mind upon will manifest in life. By concentrating upon the qualities of High Beings one is more likely to reflect those attributes in one's actions. If one is victimized by some person or agency one does not seek revenge according to the path of bhakti: you create so much power by devotion to that which is pure and right that your energy changes those who have wronged you. Positive energy affects all who contact it. Identification with all that is good and just, with the beautiful aspects of this world, with the better instincts of humanity, that is bhakti. Contemplate the beauty of a flower, a radiant sunset or a glorious full moon. Appreciation (worship) of nature is another aspect of this form of yoga. Whatever you visualize, you automatically programme into your computer. So yoga is a king of quality control mechanism. You are dealing with electricity, which is outside and inside of you. The electrical current is energized by thought. Therefore, when you project something upon your inner screen or when you concentrate upon an image (positive or negative), that picture is recorded and becomes part of your computer film bank. Every cell of brain and body is fed from that information and manifests according to the programme. You are literally transforming yourself every second that you live. This gives some idea of the importance of positive thought to physical and psychological health.

There is no doubt that conventional medicine has made great contributions to the healing arts. Miraculous surgical techniques that save lives and emergency treatments that eradicate serious disease cannot be ignored. Yoga does not reject anything which is helpful and valid to life and growth. But no single system has dominion over the realm of health. To say that drug treatment is the only way to re-establish health is both unwise and incorrect. As it is, people have come to believe somewhat religiously that they can forget about taking care of themselves, that there will be a cure for them if anything goes wrong. To teach preventive medicine is still uncommon.

One of the first recorded systems of medicine, the *Ayurveda*, was compiled thousands of years ago during the Vedic Age. This great treatise on the functions of the body contains the basis for nature cure and many other methods of curative treatments including alchemy.

Its famous sister authority, *Rig Veda*, deals with all aspects of the mind, being the more evolved ancestor of modern psychology. Higher knowledge and wisdom are propounded there. Plato's plea "Know Thyself", was a direct descendant of the teachings of the rishis. Few realize today that the principles of physics anatomy and biology were known to beings so long ago that we may, indeed, be a much more primitive civilization than that which existed before. Ancient cultures were not without communication, and the teachings of these great books spread throughout what we think of today as China, Egypt, Greece, the Roman and Persian Empires. The systems of treatment evolved into what we now call alternative medicine or holistic health maintenance which, as the name implies, considers the wellness of the whole being; physically, mentally, psychologically and spiritually. These systems are becoming increasingly popular in industrialized countries due to growing dissatisfaction with the dominance of conventional medicine.

As the Vedic teachings were expanded and brought into actual experiment and experience by the Greeks, Hippocrates propounded his wonderful oath. He told physicians exactly what principles and ethics they must assume within their practice. He would be shocked to see how medicine has evolved, both technologically and ethically in Kali Yuga. Whenever one religion, one philosophy, one system, one political movement begins to assert its totalitarian approach over truth, distortion results. Nothing should be rejected. Human justice, like the human mind, is relative as long as ego is involved. Absolute power corrupts absolutely. Yet despite harrassment and ridicule there is a revival of systems once repressed. The system of acupuncture is an example of an effective method of treatment now accepted in many countries.

Of course such cures take time. One cannot expect a chronic ailment of ten or fifteen years' curation to leave immediately. It may take a year or more of consistent treatments to eradicate illness. On the other hand, a headache can be removed instantly. There are not side effects as in drug therapy, which often removes the symptom and allows the real problem to go unseen. Chemical substances can further endanger health. Moreover, patients with a 'terminal' illness sometimes find relief from symptoms which would otherwise have to be handled with powerful drugs that would make their normal activities impossible. It is good that such patients are being given some choice these days as to forms of treatment.

There are seventy-two thousand nerves spread through the body and all must be in proper function if the person is to remain healthy. Balance of this intricate machinery, the human nervous system, is easily upset by outside agents like additives in food and polluted air and water as well as by inside agents of negative thought and emotion. As a result it becomes distorted and diseased. Herbal treatment combined with an exercise programme to suit the individual's temperament can be very effective. Since the nerves are an electrical system which affect every organ in the body, it is imperative that they be considered in any treatment. One of the most effective therapies, therefore, is management of prana (Life force) and of thought, as propounded by the system of yoga. For thought is electrically charged and prana is that very energy which heals, vitalizes and supports life.

In yoga, movement, unity and balance are emphasized. If you are tired, you relax. If you are tense and concerned with a problem, focus your energy there and let the tension release itself. Do not take care of one aspect of your being and neglect the others. Learn to relate the most subtle influences in your environment to your feelings and thoughts. There is constant transformation in everything. When food moves through the intestines, for instance, the digestive processes go to work, blood circulates, energy is divided, mixed and changed into new forms. Substances are created to fit the body's needs. The energy is used in thinking, walking, sleeping; in every seemingly passive state constant transmutation takes place. Unless the spine is kept supple, the precious substances it creates cannot be released into the system. The spine is, after all, the pillar and basic foundation of mind and body. It is the vital link between thought, nerves, senses and organs. The spinal cord is the main exchange route for so many important messages. This area receives tremendous attention in the more advanced forms of yoga due to the movement of the Kundalini Shakti (coiled serpent power) through this channel. For now, let it suffice that the movement of the spine creates essential properties within the healthy physical being. Stagnation and inertia are detrimental to yogic growth.

Mother Nature, the balancer, takes her course. Hers is such a complex and powerful way that human wilfulness has no chance. If you work in harmony with her, she will protect you; if you abuse her care and bounty, she will teach you – maybe through much pain and suffering – until the human being has learned to respect her laws.

In India it is said there are nine kinds of Mother:

Brahmani gives birth to all creation:
Lakshmi looks after us, providing wealth, prosperity;

Saraswati gives knowledge;
Durga disciplines;
Uma helps us become wise and enlightened;
Parvati represents stability, mindfulness, balance;
Vaisnavi gives liberation;
Chandi is our protectress.

Then there is Kali, whose black, naked body is adorned with humans skulls and whose eyes are red and fiery. In one hand she holds a sword, in the other fire. Blood drips from her protruding tongue. This aspect manifests to sort things out when nothing else works. When human beings behave like demons, neglecting to respect their position within the system of nature, she takes this course of action causing disaster and natural calamities. There is a story about the revenge of Kali. Most of the humans have been destroyed already. Those innocent few who are left go to Shiva and say, "You are the other half of Kali. Please help." "No, I am the other half of Parvati. When she is at this stage, I can do nothing to stop her." Still, Shiva goes into the forest, where he knows Kali is about to come, and he lies upon the path, covered with foliage. Everything is destroyed as Kali proceeds. But when she steps upon the body of Shiva, she feels skin and it reminds her of her affection for her children. Engulfed in her own motherliness, she turns into Parvati.

We must never forget that the aspect which created and nurtured us can also destroy us if we get out of control. We must realize who and what we are, giving up our ignorance and egocentric behaviour. We must not forget how shortsighted and limited human beings are. Otherwise, we are doomed.

On the contrary, when you promote those attributes and qualities that you have inherited from your Higher Self, planting peace and compassion in your environment – when you implement the teachings of Poorna Yoga within your life – you become a moving messenger of higher energy. You influence every creature you contact with your positive energy. At times it may seem that your efforts are not rewarded. But that is for nature to decide. Her workings cannot be totally comprehended by human minds. Eventually you will witness our own enlightenment. When the right time comes, what is already working silently and invisibly within you will unfold. Meantime, do not get depressed or disappointed. Right effort and positive karma will cause growth. When the being you really are begins to emerge, all confusion, all fear and all sorrow will drop away from you. You will see clearly where you belong. You belong to no nation, no culture, no race, no philosophy, no social system. Identification is a question of conditioning and environment; a mere trick of perception, which is limited. You are not limited. You either belong nowhere or everywhere. You start to see your own play – your lila – and you move through life unmoved, unattached. You are always exactly who and what you are. Complete.

8

Seeking the Lotus within

A lotus takes birth
'Midst clay and stagnant ponds
Standing clear and sound
Of clinging mud and water
Sunwards bound
Awaiting its time . . .
Preparing the ground . . .
It opens at dawn,
Brilliance abound,
Flowering of purity
Eternal sound
Manifestation of truth
Of being, newly found

SVAMI PŪRṆĀ

According to legend, Brahma found himself sitting on a lotus pod at the centre of nothingness which would become the universe. He wondered, "Where did I come from . . who am I . . . what is my root, my source . . . how did I come to be . . . what am I to do? He searched all of eternity for his roots, for ultimate reality, and when he did not find that, exhausted and perplexed, he withdrew into samadhi. Gradually he became aware of a sound, a sound which filled every cell of his being with bliss, the eternal, cosmic sound. And as he merged with the sound, he heard the message, "Brahma, you be Creator, you create . . . ."

That knowledge of Brahman, the Ultimate, heard in samadhi by Brahma, the Creator, is called 'sruti'. It was the source of the Vedas. This same sound was heard by Kabir, the great saint and philosopher. He said, "Don't you hear the sound which goes on and on within yourself? That flute whose beautiful melody fills you, that drum which beats its constant cadence within the depth of you? Remove the curtain of your heart and see the Beloved sitting inside yourself. Close your ears to the outside and hear the cosmic sound going on within you." Mira, poet-saint of Rajasthan, also spoke of that beauty inside, singing the praise of the creator. "The beloved of other people is outside, a stranger from a foreign country. My Beloved dwells in my heart; I am in his presence every moment of my life."

How can you find that music? It is the sound of the Ultimate, and you must seek it with all your heart. Samadhi, as described by Patanjali, is the eighth and highest step in the eight-fold path, the final level of consciousness. It is the union with Brahman. From that vantage point the whole ocean seems but a drop of water whose source is a cosmic river running from the sky. The sun is a great charioteer, driving his chariot around the cosmos. Those who know the mystery of the cosmos become the cosmos. All the suns, planets and stars become part of you as you understand: "Brahman, great cosmic being, you are in my heart; you are king of my soul; you are in me and around me . . . creator, preserver and dissolver. You are the lover of solitude, very far, yet very near . . . the tiniest and the biggest, living in every atom and cell, in galaxies and eternities. Let me become what I truly am, ascending and descending to watch the creation as a play of my own. You are in me and I am in you."

You cannot just jump into samadhi or take it like a drug which instantly 'enlightens', yet it is possible that this may be bestowed spontaneously. In general, you will grow in the right direction if you follow certain disciplines mindfully.

Remind yourself that creative energy is in all of nature, including you. Be aware in every thought and action you perform that you are expressing some particle, however minute, of the Infinite which works through you. You are a medium for cosmic expression. Think: "Let every moment of mine be creative and wise, let my breath be nourishing to my heart. As I inhale cosmic energy, let my body and mind be purified, my mind become sharp as a sword, my knowledge as vibrant as fire. Let all aspects of me become higher, so that this body and mind will serve to further my evolution. Then I will, with great reverence and gratitude, offer back what nature has given me."

Everything is Brahman. Therefore, whatever goes into the

body or mind is part of that and becomes part of us. We must assimilate knowledge as well as food, discarding that which is useless and taking in only that which will bring us closer to fulfilment. Some say that it does not matter what you eat, you may eat the most rotten substances and still grow, if the mind is attuned to higher energy. That may be possible, but it is not probable. Decay is part of the law of matter. If you are sincerely seeking growth, you will assert yourself positively in every aspect of your life. To become pure and positive, one should think, act and speak, even eat in a pure and positive manner. Do not confine yourself behind a wall of negative manifestations such as anger, hatred, greed, envy and prejudice, but lift yourself above that. "I am everything, I am the cosmos and the cosmos is within me; whatever is pure and positive I am That!" Remove the negative aspects, the obsessions and neuroses from your sphere of existence. Break the boundaries of limited mind and body. Experience bliss throughout yourself and around yourself. Find yourself in the Ultimate . . . you are above, in the highest state of consciousness. It is possible to live outside the law of matter.

Like Brahma, you do not become attached. You are not sorrowful at the passing of the past. You do what is necessary for growth and you forget the rest. Once the purpose is served, the creator dissolves creation. He goes to sleep for twelve hours, which are long hours by earthly time measurement. The sleep of Brahma equals the time span of the four yugas combined and takes place at the end of kali yuga. When he awakens, the sun rises, and once more he begins to create. Such creation has the quality of a child building sandcastles on the beach, then dissolving them with a sweep of the hand and starting over the next day. Creating in the morning and wiping away at the end of the day. Enjoying and building, then destroying without the slightest remorse, for a new creation will take its place. There is beauty in this constant creativity, not sadness. What was there yesterday is gone today. Each moment is gone as soon as it comes. Why be sad when you recognize the inevitability of it all?

Two men were carrying their loved one's body to cremate it

on the riverbank. The body was placed on the pyre, the fire was lit, and the two sat and watched it burn. One was quite beside himself with grief. The other just contemplated the meaning of death and remained calm. No complaining, no remorse, no crying or lamenting. That is the way to take life's experiences, as they come, without attachment to anything. One gains wisdom from observation, feeling part of nature and being receptive to all her lessons.

Learning is not dependent upon what happens to you, but on how you deal with it. Perception is important. What may seem hardship to one person is joy to another. Isolation or loneliness is considered a great torture by many; the worst prisoners are put into solitary confinement as punishment. Yet some yogis and sages find great bliss in that aloneness. It is a chance to come closer to God. They may live in caves for years without seeing or speaking to a soul. They may be at altitudes where there are no animals, where nothing grows. They live solely in the presence of the Beloved inside. Contemplate on that and try to understand why this is possible for some and inconceivable for others.

Fasting, contemplation, meditation, yoga asanas and various other disciplines can be difficult. Observation of oneself, integrity and morality can be a challenging path. If you take it well, there is no hardship. But if you approach your growth half-heartedly, you will only go backward. Each mistake will take you back. Doubt especially will dissipate any energy you have gathered through your efforts. You cannot be passive, there must be movement in one direction or another. If you grow, you go forward into higher realms of experience. If you do not grow, you waste your energy. You have to observe yourself carefully and try to understand how you block your own growth by thought, speech and action. Many people forget the difference between ego and determination. That is a trap. It is a modern concept that without ego nothing will work. In truth, without determination nothing works. Ego is a negative distortion of that. Ego thinks only of itself and denies the existence of others. It is not concerned with the sufferings of others so long as it is happy. That attitude is not determination, nor the willingness to sacrifice, nor the resolution to reach the goal at the expense of one's own comfort. If you are really free, you do not disturb the freedom of others with your freedom. True freedom is being prepared to grow beyond the confines of one's ego and its self-imposed limitations.

The same human being that boasts, "I am this and I am that," gets a chill and expires. It cannot even hold a temperature of 105°F without wilting. It just dies. Life is fragile. Those who are very materialistic are unable to see this, but an aura of energy which protects and sustains is built around one who seeks the Ultimate wholeheartedly. Through spiritual disciplines you begin to accumulate energy which will eventually become noticeable. Maya supports positivity. If you can maintain a positive vibration, nature will take care of you . . . Mother Nature arranges everything for you. But unless you take the first steps, she cannot take you further. Do not be satisfied with little things when you can accomplish great things. How can you compromise with less than you are? You are whole, total, complete. Can you sacrifice the highest value, the most fulfiling knowledge, for small, material accomplishments? Remember, you are everything or you are nothing; if you are everything, then your heart is so big it can hold all of humanity within itself, you have no jealousy or narrowness. You are in the heart of every creature and every creature is in your heart. There is only bliss. That height will be achieved when your body is engaged in the performance of good actions, your mind is filled with devotion, and your entire self is eagerly pursuing knowledge. As gold is purified in fire, so the fires of discipline and austerity cleanse and purify the seeker. By karma yoga the physical body is transmuted to a higher vibration. Mind and heart are cleansed and the emotions transformed to the higher attribute of humble devotion through bhakti yoga. By jnana yoga the psyche is enlightened, one profound in knowledge can withdraw the mind in knowledge. A hatha yogi is "one who has complete control over sun and moon". That is the literal Sanskrit meaning. It means control over every aspect of the body;

inhalation and transmission of energy throughout the nervous system through the practice of pranayama and various kriyas, as well as mental control of the organs. Very advanced hatha yogis can defy the dictates of so-called normal biological laws. They employ body techniques to go beyond the body, and to do that they have necessarily involved the mind as an organ of that body. Thus one can see that even hatha yoga, which begins with body, leads into higher aspects of consciousness. The body is only a tool, a vehicle.

A yogi may employ more tangible means, such as herbal and mineral treatments. He may use Rasayana, which is a technique of utilizing various metals which have been specially treated, to effect a subtle transformation of the physical and mental bodies. Very few yogis are knowledge-able in Rasayana Shastra. Though some know how to prepare the metals, only those very spiritually advanced are able to use them to full benefit. As willing alchemists have found, many alchemical formulas simply do not work unless the alchemist is able to maintain a positive vibration. To obtain results does not merely depend on mixing certain chemical compounds. Yet even for that work a certain degree of evolution is required. Finally, when it comes to taking the compounds, one must be prepared beforehand. People are looking for a pill that will make them young forever. But how many would be able to tolerate this pill if it existed? Yogis not only ingest mercury and other heavy metals, generally considered lethal, they are also not harmed by poisonous bites. They can survive on a minimum of air, food and water for very long periods. They seem to be immune to extremes of temperatures. By such methods, yogis overcome attachment to the body and build power of will.

Physical perfection is not unattainable. But the final and highest attainment is that state where lower laws merge into the higher. It has to do with transformation of consciousness. It is complex transmutation into what may be termed spiritual immortality. The eventual destruction of all matter – the law of Pralaya – is a hard law of physics. But cosmic law supersedes all else. One who is incapable of understanding may perceive miracles; but once the principles behind the manifestation are understood, there is no more mystery.

There is no one technique that will guarantee your growth. You should explore every avenue and technique, passing through on your way towards your goal, within the matrix of your own karma. As you proceed, it is helpful to let go of all conditioning. Remember that you have your own type of alchemy going on within you. By knowledge, you can transform your own body chemistry. That is a subtle art. Thousands of chemicals are produced by your thoughts, emotions, feelings and actions. Spiritual striving creates a healing effect upon your glands and organs, which respond by producing healthful chemicals. Negativity, such as anger, jealousy and so on, creates poisonous substances within every cell. Contemplate on the responsibility that you can create or destroy. As you grow in knowledge, the physical body will transform in accordance with your new state of consciousness.

One of many ways towards growth is through association with a High Being or true Guru. One greatly benefits by implementing the teachings of such a Being. It may be enjoyable just to be in his company, to have his grace, but that alone simply will not get you to the Ultimate Goal. Make the most of the teachings at every moment. If your mind is not clear, you cannot see your own reflection. When you are full of doubt, confusion and desire, you will not hear the teachings. If your mind and heart are disturbed by negative emotions, or if you are not sure what you want, you cannot receive the energy the guru sends . . . you miss your chance to enter another dimension of your being. You must relax, let your soul relax, open your heart and mind to the flow of Cosmic Energy, the nectar which dwells within you. You lose nothing, on the contrary, you have everything to gain. There is nothing you can offer the Infinite except the flower of your heart. By humility, by surrendering the ego, you eventually transform the body into a higher state of consciousness and create a candle-like aura.

The mind is a rider of wild horses, the senses. The body is the carriage. You sit and are driven into a ditch or are transported to your goal. The idea is to reach your destination safely and soundly, not to get stuck along the way. There is no way out of that ditch of karma that causes you to be born again and again, except to pass through it mindfully, without mourning, suffering, lamenting, reacting. Remain neutral, as an observer above it all. Life should be fulfilling, never a burden. Things happen because they are supposed to, due to individual and collective karma. It does no good to try to deny your responsibilities. Watch creation pass before you without becoming involved.

Yogis train to overcome fear. For what is there to fear? Destruction of the body is not destruction of consciousness. And anyone who fears is displaying body-consciousness. The thought that "I am this body" creates fear. Secondary fears such as not having means to survive or other insecurities are still results of a distorted sense of self. Fear that another will die or be harmed is also a symptom of attachment and duality. As long as one is on the path, there is nothing to fear. You will not be destroyed, for Maya responds lovingly to the positive vibration of genuine devotion and truth-seeking.

Depression is not always negative. It can be the result of awakening energy. Sometimes so much energy is built up that there can be pain or the feeling that a current is flowing through the body. Spiritual longing and frustration may seem like depression, but it is a positive thing. This energy can be activated at any age – a four-year-old child asking questions about life's meaning or needing to run and move about for no special reason may be reacting to this awakening power within the spine. There is no time limit or formula to growth; it is individual and unique to every creature.

In order to grow, you need sraddha, bhakti and seva. They are the basic qualifications. Sraddha is faith, bhakti is devotion, seva is service.

If you are not attuned to your guru, you cannot receive the energy. If your faith is weak, if you are uncertain and in-decisive about what you want, you will prevent your own growth. Stability of emotions and mind are essential to grow further. As you go through any test or trial, do not question the motives of the teacher or preceptor. Everyone is taught differently, according to individual karma or need. Accept everything positively.

If you are miserable, how can you make someone else happy? If you are unclean, how can you create cleanliness? If you are confused, how can you radiate clarity? If you are in darkness, how can you create light? Everything that happens has meaning. Never take it as accident. There are no accidents in spiritual life, and no coincidences. Everything is built and determined by karma. When an opportunity to grow presents itself, you should take full advantage of this moment. It will not be coming again in the same form. Do not slow your progress by unmindful acts, doubt and instability. You cannot work out your karma by avoidance.

Just being a seeker makes you different from most people. But that is not enough. It is a rough journey you have decided to make. Every day, week, month and year you must go forward. You need courage, determination and unending perseverance. High beings are like rivers, whose virtue is to flow; like trees, whose virtue is to fruit; like the sun, whose virtue is to shine; and like the earth, whose virtue is to nourish and support.

Examine whether you have the qualities that are basic to growth: mindfulness, self-observation, non-violence, forbearance . . . ? Realize that on the cosmic level all of you are one. On the worldly level try to maintain harmony, unity, integrity and respect for one another. By obstructing another, you block your own growth. If you do not understand, knowledge is necessary. If you do not feel the energy, devotion is necessary. If you cannot communicate, service is necessary. You can communicate beyond time and distance if you search within the lotus of your heart. You will be guided if you are receptive to the teachings. But for a map to be of use, you need to follow it. You are entering new territory, the realm of the spirit. If you are able to perceive this lotus within your heart, Himalayan vision will be revealed to you.

There once lived an evil-tempered cobra who had developed a nasty habit of biting everyone who chanced his way. Many people had died, and nearby villagers lived in fear of crossing his path. One day a yogi was passing through the woods when the cobra approached him menacingly. "What do you want?" enquired the yogi. "To bite you, of course!" replied the serpent. "Indeed, have you not done enough harm to others and to yourself already? Don't you realize that one day you will have to pay for all your actions?" Having said this, the yogi turned away, ignoring the cobra, and settled himself into meditation. Hours later, when the yogi opened his eyes, the cobra was still there, waiting. "Please, Holy Sir, while you meditated I have been thinking. I am truly sorry for all the suffering I have caused. Could you help me and tell me how to make up for all my misdeeds?" So the yogi initiated the cobra and told him that although he would indeed have to undergo suffering for his evils of the past, he should stop biting and killing.

A year had passed when the yogi returned. He went looking for his unusual disciple despite convincing rumours that the cobra must surely be dead. Stories were told of the cruel treatment the snake had received from the village boys after they discovered that he would no longer bite. Eventually the yogi found the cobra, in dreadful condition, emaciated, lame and covered with sores.

"Whatever happened to bring you to this pitiful condition?" he questioned his disciple. The cobra, so purified by his earnest efforts to improve, had almost forgotten the harsh treatment he had suffered at the hands of the boys. He replied that it must be his unaccustomed diet of roots and berries which had made him so weak. Only when the yogi reminded him of the youths did the cobra remember. "Ah, yes, the boys did get a little excited, but then you had told me to be kind."

The yogi reflected silently for a moment, then spoke softly to his disciple, "I instructed you not to bite, I didn't say, 'Don't hiss . . . !'"

The gentle humour of this story should not let us forget its lesson. It is not enough to listen attentively to the instructions of any teacher. A student who really wants to make progress will implement these instructions faithfully and mindfully, not blindly. The teachings of the prophets and saints are always clear and positive. It is their followers who interpret thoughts according to their own state of mind. Consequently, the meaning becomes very different to that expounded by the masters. The tendency to assume or to interpret everything the way one would like it to be will only bring more suffering. If you contemplate the teachings, you will understand them.

Meditation will help to clarify things. It makes the mind more receptive. Mind is always active and moving and it can be difficult to bring it to stability. It is like a monkey jumping from branch to branch. Mind goes from one thought to another, ceaselessly. There is a right and a wrong time to attempt meditation. Usually, in the morning just after awakening is a receptive time. You get up, wash your face and sit in lotus or other comfortable posture. The evening, just prior to sleep, is also good, for the mind is ready to relax. The wrong time is when you are especially agitated, when your mind is disturbed and under the influence of rajaguna or tamaguna (frantic activity or negativity). Your efforts will be frustrating and fruitless. But when the restless, tired mind is weary of thought and craves silence, that is the time to give it what it wants . . . rest . . . quiet . . . solitude. Then your mind will go effortlessly into the meditative state you have been trying to bring about. Learn to listen to your inner voice. Everything will happen when the time is right. Even samadhi will come. If you have done the preparation, it will be revealed to you. You cannot force growth. That is the great mystery, how creation develops, and you along with it.

It is essential to maintain balance in body, mind and soul. Just as you need balanced nutrients to nourish the body, you need certain elements to nourish the soul. In the same way, if you let your emotions take you wherever they wish, you will be malnourished spiritually and you will have wasted the same energy that might have taken you to your goal.

This is how you begin to seek the lotus within.

9
"But Guruji . . ."

If one has supreme love for God
And also loves his master as God
Then the light of his teaching
Shines in a great soul
It shines indeed in a great soul.

SVETASVATARA UPANISHAD

Some people say that they are searching for truth. But this is mostly pretence. If not, one would not be disappointed when faced with the truth. People ask their friends, "Please tell me the truth." Yet, when told the truth, they get hurt. Why? Because no one really wants to accept reality. It seems easier to continue under the cloak of illusion. Reality destroys the charade.

Reality, however, cannot be avoided forever. The time will come when you are dissatisfied with everything that life as you have known it has to offer. You have seen, heard, tasted and enjoyed all, yet happiness and contentment have eluded you. Then you may begin to look for a deeper, more profound meaning of life. Many of you have gone from religious orders to spiritual organizations. All this is necessary preparation and testing. At the moment of complete exhaustion, when the sincere has been sorted from the false, along comes the real Master and, being a reflection of the Self which abides in each creature, the genuine seeker will instinctively be attracted to him.

At this point you may ask, "But how can I be sure of the Master's authenticity?" You may be assured that the real Master, the true Guru (meaning dispeller of the darkness of ignorance) will know exactly how to let you experience who and what He is.

The high energy which the guru transmits effects a turnover in the aspirant's personality. Every hidden thought, desire and quality comes to the surface, both good and bad. For some time it may even appear that the aspirant presents over-whelming negativities (reminiscent of the old proverb that when you are surrounded by alligators, it is difficult to remember that your initial objective was to drain the swamp). Yet, this cleansing process is absolutely necessary for the purification of body, mind and soul. The idea is to catch what-ever 'mud' comes up and to remove it promptly, before it can sink again. Thus it will trouble you no more.

It seems, however, that instead of mastering the difficulty, you become its victim time and again. It is necessary for you to understand that whatever you see or perceive is the product of mind. Mind is one of the four aspects of the subtle body, the others being intellect, ego and emotion. Though essentially one, while manifesting separately, these four will do their work. Ego lurks in every thought, often backed by emotion. With the aid of this unstable couple, mind will create and rule you. Intellect, the adviser, is mostly ignored. It is your decision to be the victim of these instincts, or their master. In the big ego/emotional ocean you lose all control of yourself. One moment you are being flung up, riding on a big wave, and nearly drowning the next, in constant fluctuation. There is no balance, there is no stability. Programmed by previous conditioning and present environment, the four instincts of the subtle body will influence you to project the unstable consciousness of the outside world and will dictate your life.

To be able to assimilate and understand higher truths, these instincts must be purified. Only through purification can mastery be achieved. When motivated by a real longing to find your Source, to find freedom, knowledge, love and light, you recognize the necessity of this process. There should be no problem at all. Yet, what happens along the way? You forget. As soon as you experience the slightest attack on your ego, you react so strongly that you forget all the beautiful aspira-tions, forget your direction and your goal, and you forget the purpose and role of your guru. This kind of forgetfulness and ignorance often leads to behaviour totally unsuitable to the situation of a spiritual aspirant. It belies and belittles the sacred relationship between guru and disciple – between God and the Soul.

The first and second limbs of Patanjali's Eight-Fold Path of Yoga outline certain observations and restrictions, disciplines and rules that promote cleansing of the personality, thus providing a basis for further growth. Discipline is absolutely vital. If I ask you to undergo any kind of discipline, it is because this is good for you; it will help your development. Yet, you object. You may object most respectfully, "Yes, Guruji, I will do this, but . . ." Still there is something in you which revolts. You try to find a way around the situation. I may ask you not to watch television for some time (knowing that this will only distract you from other duties and activities). ". . . but Guruji, it's all right to watch the news or a documentary, isn't it? It's educational . . . ." When I instruct you not to eat for a day or two to cleanse your system and thoughts from impurities, what is the reply? " . . . but Swamiji, I must eat something or I will be weak, I might faint . . . ." Are these the reflections of mature, striving souls? Is it asking too much to cut out television or a few meals for the sake of higher growth? These are the most simple, basic disciplines which you should think of yourself. Until you have learned to transmute every aspect of life into positivity, you will have to rely on the guru's judgement. But the problem is again that you forget the purpose of my instructions. Do I teach and train you for my benefit? Nevertheless, discipline and obedience from a sense of fear are equally useless, for where there is fear, love cannot coexist. True discipline can never be imposed on anyone or anybody; it must spring from the heart – spontaneously.

Some of you go to the other extreme and follow the instructions more to the letter than in the essence, especially when you may be feeling somewhat contrary. As a rule you cannot follow general instructions so blindly that when the situation alters fundamentally you still go ahead with the 'instruction', possibly creating disaster, " . . . but Swamiji, you said so".

The teachings of the prophets and saints are always clear

and positive. It is their followers who interpret thoughts according to their own state of mind. Consequently, the meaning becomes very different to that expounded by the masters. When Lord Buddha taught, he did not once mention Īsvara or God because at that time atrocities and exploitations took place in the name of Īsvara. He taught Nirvāna, Enlightenment, Sublime Truth. But as he had not used the word God, people misunderstood his teachings. Seven hundred years after the Buddha's physical death, a congregation of Buddhist monks and scholars met and decided that since there was no mention of God, the Buddha did not accept the existence of God. By the decree of his own followers, the divine incarnation thus became an atheist!

There is a lighter story of an example of how mindless interpretation, wilfulness and impatience may combine into a formidable danger for the new seeker. The new disciple approached his guru and implored, "Master, please show me God." The guru replied, "My dear, God is something which must be experienced. Wait . . . ." Before he could finish, the impatient disciple interrupted, "No, no, I cannot wait; please give me something, teach me something." The sage spoke softly and patiently, "All right, if you insist, I'll give you something. Remember, God is everywhere – in you, in me, in every creature. Don't forget this truth. Try to see God everywhere and try to love everybody." The disciple jumped to his feet. "Certainly, Guruji, I cannot wait to experiment with this."

The disciple was going along the road when he noticed an elephant coming his way, and approaching very fast. "Ah, this is a good time to implement my guru's instructions," he reflected. "I am God and the elephant is God. God need not be afraid of God." He remained in the road. Now the mahout on top of the elephant started shouting, "Please, Sir, get out of the road quickly, make way for this elephant, he is mad and I cannot control him!" "Why should I?" the disciple retorted, "God need not be afraid of God."

Well, the elephant could not be stopped . . . and the new disciple received a somewhat unusual massage. He had to be admitted to the hospital with several broken bones. Guruji came to know about his disciple's plight and went to visit him. "How do you come to be in such a sorry state?" he enquired. "This is the result of your teaching; I follow it implicitly, and now look at me!" wailed the disciple. "All right, tell me exactly what happened." "Well, as I was walking, and the elephant came towards me, I remembered your teaching that God is in everything. Consequently, I was not intimidated by the elephant, who is God, too. But Guruji, he just trampled me." "Did something else happen?" "What else? Is that not enough? No . . . . only the mahout yelled at me to get out of the road." "That's it," Guruji pointed out. "You see, the mahout is also God. You did not listen to the third God!"

Life will constantly present you with opportunities to train your mind, to let it do some constructive work. If you use the tools of intellect and mind to 'reason mindfully', you can advance your own growth. So think, analyze, contemplate, and then act. As you become accustomed to this process of mindful reasoning, you also learn to recognize and direct the subtle workings of ego and emotion. Of course, mistakes can still occur, but you should learn from these. One commits mistakes to be above mistakes. Learn from your mistakes and become wise. To achieve the highest, to merge with the highest, you must become like the highest – infinite intelligence and infinite wisdom.

But how can you learn from a mistake you refuse to recognize? It seems very difficult for people to admit wrongs. Usually they try to find endless excuses to defend themselves. "But Guruji, I thought . . . I presumed . . . ·" This is something negative and destructive in everyone. What do you defend? This is only the ego in its worst manifestation. More than that, you try to blame someone or something else for your own shortcomings. " . . . but Guruji, it wasn't my fault . . . ." Again you forget that I know exactly whose fault it was. You may succeed in fooling yourself, but do not try to fool your guru. Learn to be honest with yourself, search and analyze your motives and reactions. Learn to take responsibility for your actions. You may look upon responsibility as a privilege, forgetting that first and foremost it is an obligation and a commitment.

The love of the true guru goes out to all – equally. There is no need to compete for this love, it is given freely and abundantly. How much you receive is equal to your faith and trust. The woman who touched the hem of Jesus' garment was healed because of her absolute faith in him. Being a human, your perspective is limited. The human is not able to fathom the divine motive, hence you cannot possibly assume judgement over the guru's actions, let alone criticize or complain. Try to avoid the dangers of rivalry and comparison. By focus on and comparison with others instead of tending your own garden, and by assuming censorship of your guru's decisions, you literally block the flow of love the guru sends. Ego-prompting foolish jealousies have no place in the life of one who is striving for Eternal Life. Until such thoughts and ideas have been removed from your mind completely, further growth will be effectively obstructed.

Contemplate on the effect of even the strongest light on the colour black. Does it not absorb, 'swallow' the light completely? Likewise, negativities like jealousy, anger, envy, bickering, etc. will swallow the energy and light the guru transmits. Whenever you are filled with light-absorbing negative emotions, thoughts and impulses, you resemble a bottomless pit – no matter how much energy and light the guru may pour in, it will never be filled. I ask you to consider: what is the sense in continuing such waste indefinitely? Though the guru has infinite patience and mercy, the priceless gift of spiritual energy should not be wasted and abused. Light must be reflected, to shine further.

The guru will always pay attention .to those who are prepared to discipline themselves, who really want to grow. Do you want to be close? The closest will always be the ones with the highest qualities, the purest motives. So strive, purify, evolve; constantly and incessantly. The moment you perceive your goal, the moment you realize that you must do something, every instinct and aspect of yourself must transform with only one aim – to achieve That. If you think you will

devote 'some' time of your life to your upliftment, to the ultimate goal of reaching your Source, your half-hearted efforts
will be in vain.

To one who has never been accustomed to any kind of
discipline, never attempted to control the appetites of the
senses, discipline may appear as a most difficult thing. Yet
there is another way which makes everything very easy, a
sunlit and happy path; the path of bhakti, of love and
devotion. It is said that the road of self-perfection is like love.
If one is in love, one is prepared to give up everything for the
sake of the loved one. And for the love of God this is the
requirement; for how can you discover the Infinite while still
grossly attached to the finite?

In the fifteenth century lived the great poet and saint Kabir.
Many people claimed they wanted to follow him. He had to
find a way to separate the chaff from the wheat, discern the
real seekers from the pretenders. Thus upholding the masala,
a blazing torch, he proclaimed that he would accept as
disciples all those who were prepared to first burn their
houses. It worked. Excuses and withrawals abounded. However, before giving rise to further misunderstandings, Kabir
did not entice anyone to literally commit arson; he asked them
to give up their attachments to the material world. In many of
his beautiful and heart-rending poems Kabir reminds us, "I
tell you the ways of love . . . even though the head must be
given, why should you weep over it?" Jesus also admonishes
that the pearl of great price can only be obtained by "selling all
you have".

If you want to follow the path of bhakti, pure devotion will
transform your energy; God/Guru becomes your Beloved.
You relate to him by faith and trust. You present yourself as
you are, with all your imperfections. You tell him all your sins.
But once you have said all that you are, once you have been
accepted and graced by God, you are no longer a sinner and
there is no need to repeat the statement. You have told God,
and God does not suffer from forgetfulness.

The encounter between the old woman Sabari and Lord
Rama illustrates this relationship beautifully when Sabari

asks, "Oh my Lord, how could you accept someone like me, an old and outcast woman? I, who am full of disease, rejected by society, ignorant and ugly. How could you accept me?" Lord Rama replies, "You have taken my refuge, there is no difference between you and Me. What I am, you are; and what you are, I am." Thus, once you have taken shelter at the feet of the Highest, once your emotions are purified, you are no longer a sinner. If you truly realize who and what you are, you do not have to repeat every now and again, ". . . but Guruji, you are so high and I am still the sinner."

Is is sad that some religious denominations promote the repeated affirmations of such negative statements. If you repeat all your life that you are the sinner, will that lead you to enlightened bliss? Of course not; it will merely produce guilty consciousness. Why should you feel guilty? You are not wicked, cruel and miserable. A great thought to annihilate guilt is, "How can I be guilty, when I am your devotee?" Rather think that you are happy, blissful, pure and good – not only think so, but contemplate, live and identify with these qualities. Build them into your life that they may take root, grow and bloom. When you merge into these particles of perfection, when you realize who and what you really are, you will no longer be what you used to be.

There is a story which tells about such a transformation. It was a warm summer's evening. The people of the little Indian village had been busy all day preparing for the great event of the night. A pandit, a priest, famous for his brilliant and inspiring tales of deities and saints, had arrived to give a discourse at a wealthy man's home, and everybody was invited. Many people had gathered outside the house and now listened with rapt attention to various events taken from the life of Krishna.

There was one man, not part of the general audience, who thought this evening the ideal moment to promote his 'trade'. He was a thief. What better opportunity to rob the wealthy man's house than at this time, when everyone was busy listening to Panditji. Careful not to make any noise, he proceeded to make an opening in the side of the house. This was a slow and tedious job, and while thus engaged, he could not help over-hearing the priest's talk. Just now Panditji was giving an account of Lord Krishna's beauty and splendour, and how he would play heart-rending tunes on his flute, surrounded by cows and the adoring cow-herds and milkmaids. The thief, who had no idea who and what Krishna represented, was not much impressed. However, when he heard all about the beautiful ornaments and precious jewels which adorned Krishna, he suddenly had an idea. "What am I doing here, robbing a few things from each house?" he thought. "If I were to rob this Krishna, all my problems would be over. I would not have to rob every now and then. But, how to find him?"

The discourse had come to an end and everybody had gone home. Panditji, too, was on his way home. Suddenly, out of the dark, the thief jumped right into Panditji's path. The priest was terrified. "Don't kill me," he pleaded. "Take whatever you want, but don't kill me."

"Panditji, I don't want to kill you," said the thief. "All I want is the address of this Krishna you have been talking about. You give me the address, and I shall leave you in peace."

The priest could not believe his ears. Could anyone really be such a fool as to take such stories seriously? However, he concluded that there was no point in arguing with a madman. In order to appease the robber, he told him that although he did not have the precise address, he would surely find him in Brindaban.

The robber set out for Brindaban, where several thousand years ago Krishna had dwelt. There was nothing in his mind but the treasure, soon to be his. So absorbed did he become in the meditation on gold and jewels that he wandered here and there . . . and completely lost the way. Yet visualizing all the ornaments on Krishna, how could he avoid visualizing his face, also, his eyes, his mouth, his hair? That complete con-centration brought him into such attunement with the vibration of Krishna that he was not aware of anything else any longer. He became totally absorbed in the high energy emanated by Krishna – in Krishna Consciousness. In the fire of this energy all his sins burnt away; body, mind and soul became so purified that he began to 'see'. He saw the forest, the river, tulsi trees; he began to see Brindabran. Finally, when he heard the distant ring of cowbells, and high above that the jubilant trill of a flute, he knew that Krishna was approaching. Hidden in the branches of a large tree, his excitement became paramount when he finally discerned Krishna in a group of people and cows. Recognizing his clothes, hair and jewels – oh, those jewels – the flute lightly to his lips, the thief could barely contain himself until, alighting from the branch, he jumped in front of Krishna and informed him of his intention to rob him.

Krishna tried to dissuade him, "No, you can't do that, you can't rob me. These jewels are not mine. They belong to my mother. What will I tell her if you take everything away?" Krishna, of course, was referring to Mother Nature, to whom all worldly goods belong. Nonetheless, although by now a pure being, the robber was still attached to what he had come for. He insisted on his spoils, and in trying to snatch them, there was a current . . . a flash . . . his mind and body were suddenly flooded with infinite light. Ultimate understanding filled him.

He stepped back in awe. "No, Lord, I want nothing. I want nothing but to carry this moment in my heart." But now Krishna informed him that since the treasure had been his motive, since this was what he had come for, he must now take it. There was no way out. At the moment of enlightenment, Mother Nature had become the robber's servant, ready to grant him everything. Yet, knowing that now he had everything, he wanted nothing. Reluctantly he took gold and jewels, Krishna helping him to put on the heavy crown, and he went on his way to carry his burden to Panditji's house.

As the priest opened the door, he was shocked. He could not understand when the treasure of Krishna was laid before him as his own. He did not have the slightest idea that anyone could actually meet this Being. "Where did you get this? What did you do? How could you ever . . . ?" His questions as to where and how the thief had found Krishna were endless.

With shining eyes, the former thief replied, "Panditji, how

can I explain to you? I see him all around me, I found him in everything, I found him in my very heart." Poor Panditji, no matter how hard he tried, he just could not 'see'.

This story provides just one example of the transforming and purifying effect of divine grace. The robber's motives had been anything but pure, he had determined to commit a crime. He was also an ignorant man. Before Panditji's lecture he had never even heard of Krishna. Consequently, he was quite unaware that he was dealing with divinity. Almost by 'accident' he concentrated on one aspect of the divine, yet he became absolved from all sins, a completely transformed being – Divinity Itself.

I would ask you to consider now how much more can be achieved by conscious, all-absorbing concentration on all aspects of the Ultimate, rather than its physical manifestations alone.

Sometimes it may appear that the devotees' often intense love is centred more on the finite physical form of the spiritual preceptor than on Ultimate truth. Attracted by the high radiation of pure love and compassion which the guru emits, the form is taken for the essence. This is a very common mistake for the human being. The same mistake – attachment to the physical form – is responsible for many religious misconceptions and aberrations. If people could only learn to look at all religions with an open mind, they would soon realize that essence/truth never changes. Each religion originates from a higher state of consciousness. Those that follow, however, being more limited, devalue what was once whole and pure. The human mind alone produces the differences.

There is nothing wrong with loving the physical form of your God or Guru, be that Krishna, Jesus Christ, Rama, Buddha, Mohammed, or a living Master. Remember, though, that the purpose of God's descent into human form is to communicate with you, to help you understand and experience the truth. Do not become so attached to that form that you obstruct your own growth. By remaining in one thought you will bar yourself from the reality of truth which encompasses all.

Constant reminiscences and projected fantasies will cloud and distort your outlook and keep your consciousness tied down. True devotion and service, on the other hand, will help you outgrow the boundaries of limited love. If, by loving another human being, you can become a better and kinder person, think what contact with the redeeming and trans- forming energy of God – of Cosmic love – can accomplish.

When with childlike love and trust you follow your Master's teaching, faithfully acknowledging him in every respect of your life, no situation you may encounter will present a problem to you, no task will be unpleasant or impossible. You may not understand the reason behind some instructions, yet if you can maintain the attitude, "I really don't understand, but Guruji, you know what is best . . ." then you will have dis- covered the way of Mira and Prahlad, two of the greatest lovers of God. You will have found the way to lead you out of the confines of mind, ego and emotion. You will have dis- covered the way of bhakti. By loving the real Master with all your heart, he will teach you how to love God. Verily, there is no doubt.

Real faith does not live in words alone. It lives in actions, the actions of everyday life. Every act that you perform, walking, talking, eating, relating to others, can become a reflection of faith and devotion. True faith is unwavering; it does not permit disillusionment. When people say, "We have faith in God," where is their faith when the development of circum- stances leads them into worry, fear, disappointment and doubt? I mentioned earlier that love and fear cannot co-exist; the same applies to love and doubt.

The fire-like love and devotion Kabir speaks of may not be acquired immediately, but if you have faith and trust in God/ Guru, you will serenely await his pleasure in all matters. You do not ask him to do as you would like, but you surrender your individual wishes and desires to his infinite wisdom. "Thy will be done." You lay the burden of your ego at his feet. Your cares are his. That is bhakti, the 'winged' path. On the wings of love you soar to the Beloved.

Arati is the ritual of the evening offering when the lamps are lit. You repeat the prayer of offering and surrender. But do you mean it? When you do ārati to God or to your guru, you appeal to him as remover of pain and sorrows. You take refuge: Sharan gahun kiski – to whose feet I cling. You offer yourself totally and entirely to the omnipotent, omniscient, omnipresent in-dweller of your heart – tum antaryami. Contemplate on this the next time you feel tempted to say, " . . . But Guruji . . . ."

Glossary

Svāmi Pūrṇā's titles are in capitals.

ahinsa   Non-violence; non-injury in thought, word and deed.

ajna   Literally: command; (chakra between eyebrows).

anahata   Literally: unbeaten, unstruck; (heart chakra).

ANANDA PEETHADHISVARA   Lord of the 'pitha' ('seat' or conclave) of Ananda.

Anantshreebibhusit   Divine, light, splendour, glory, loveliness, prosperity, auspicious, fortunate, of high rank.

aparigraha   Renunciation of possessions besides essentials.

ārati   Ritual in which the seeker offers himself and beseeches God or guru to relieve him of the distress and afflictions of the world.

ashram(a)   Training school for spiritual aspirants.

atma   The Self: Immortal Soul.

Aum   Sacred and mystical syllable beginning, middle and end, highest spiritual sound and vibration. The first sound of creation. A–U–M, representing the 3 gods A–Vishnu U–Shiva M–Brahma preservation, dissolution and creation respectively. Essence of the vedas, the pranavas, aum is also called pranava.

AVADHUTA   Literally: 'Naked', 'He who has relinquished all sects and creeds'.

Avatamsaka Sutra   Elaborate treatise traditionally believed to have been rendered by the Buddha. It gives a detailed account of world perception in the enlightened state of consciousness.

avatar   A divine incarnation.

Bhagavad Purana   Sacred literature on traditional and legendary basis.

bhakti   Spiritual love and devotion.

bhakti yoga   The path of loving devotion to God – of selfless dedication to the Highest.

Brahma   Personification of God as Creator.

Brahman   God; the Divine Essence; Imperishable Creative Principle; Universal Soul.

BRAHMANISTA   'He who belongs only to Brahma'.

chakra   Energy centre in the form of a 'wheel' situated in the subtle body.

danda   A stick.

dharma   Law; duty; right conduct.

Ganesh (Ganesa) Elephant-headed symbol of wisdom and dispeller of obstacles through the implementation of the qualities of wisdom.

gopis Milkmaids of Brindaban and great devotees of Krishna.

gunas Subtle qualities, influences, moods; the three underlying principles of the manifest world: *sattva* – light and positivity; *rajas* – passion and activity; *tamas* – inertia and negativity.

guru Gu – darkness, ru – light; one who leads from the darkness of ignorance to the knowledge of light; spiritual preceptor, teacher.

Guru Granth Sacred book of the Sikh religion – also revered as the 'last guru'.

hatha yoga Ha – sun, tha – moon. Physical exercises which promote the balancing of positive and negative energies within the body.

High Being Manifestation of Godhood in human form; descending soul.

Īśvara Literally: the most capable; Supreme Being; God.

Jivatman The embodied individual soul.

Kali The Black Goddess; consort of Shiva; the Divine Mother in her destructive and cataclysmic aspect.

Kali Yuga Kali: darkness, destruction; Yuga: era, age, astronomical cycle of years. Present age of darkness and strife followed by destruction.

karma Action, work, deeds, performance: the result or effects of one's actions.

King Houn Simplification of the king's full name: Rahūgana, as related in the *Bhagavad Purana*.

Krishna Divine incarnation of Vishnu.

kriya Action or performance as a religious or spiritual discipline; rite; ceremony.

Lakshmi Consort of Vishnu; goddess of wealth and beauty.

lila Play, sport, pastime: Divine Play, divine love actively engaged in worldly affairs.

MAHĀMANDALEŚVARA Literally: 'Lord of the Great Circle'. There are five such conclaves in India. Svāmi Pūrṇá heads the one at Banaras.

Maharaj Spiritual ruler resplendant.

manipura Literally: fiery sun; (naval chakra).

mantra, mantram Concentrated energy of certain sacred sound syllables.

Maya The great illusion of the world as reality; also: Mother Nature.

mudra Gesture, sign, token.

muladara Root, basis, firmly fixed. (Chakra at base of spine).

Nada Brahman 'Vibrating with the sound of the Ultimate.'

Nadam The sound of silence.

nadi Nerve channel.

Nandi The white bull, mount of Shiva.

nirvāna Literally: extinguished, calmed; final emancipation from matter; dissolution of individual existence and re-union with the Supreme Spirit.

Om   see *Aum*

Paramatma   Ultimate Being; the Divine.

'1008'/'1108'/108'   '1' stands for the 1 God, '0' for the Whole or Brahmanda, '8' for the eight manifestations of Shiva, that He has mastered.

PARIVRAJAKACĀRYA   'The Preceptor who is always on the move' like water that retains its purity by never coming to rest.

Parvati (other names)   Also known as: Uma, Durga, Kali, Gauri, Bhavani . . .

Patanjali   Ancient logician and grammarian; author of the *Yoga Sutras*, the first systematic compilation of yogic science.

pralaya   Literally: dissolution, annihilation, reabsorption; universal dissolution.

prana   Vital life force.

pranayama   Control of vital life force.

Purna   Abundant, complete, entire, fulfilled, whole.

Rasayana Shastra   Rasa: juice, extract, essence, elixir; science of alchemy.

Rig Veda (Rg Veda)   Original and most ancient collection of spiritual wisdom in prayers and hymns.

rishi   Sage.

sadhak(a)   Spiritual aspirant; one who is disciplined.

sadhana   Spiritual practice for the purpose of upliftment, of overcoming one's human limitations; disciplines.

sahasrara (sahasradala)   Literally: a thousand petals.

samadhi   Literally: joining, union, ultimate accomplishment; highest consciousness.

samskaras   Latent, ingrained tendencies of the personality.

Sastro Bhushan   Literally: invocation, praise, recitation, jewel.

SATDARŚANACĀRYA   'The Preceptor who has mastered the six Great Schools of Indian philosophy.

shakti   Primal energy; power; strength.

Shiva (Śiva)   Personification of God as Destroyer of all negativities – Shiva brings about total annihilation of the human ego.

Śiva (other names)   Maha-deva; Shankara; Maheshwar; Isa Hara; Nataraj, the Cosmic Dancer.

Śivā   Feminine aspect of Śiva.

siddhasana   Hatha yoga pose; the perfect pose.

Sivamarga   Siva's path; final liberation.

SRIMAT PARAMAHAMSA   Literally: 'The Divine Swan': 'He who is ever discriminating, but spontaneously so'.

svadhistana   Literally: having a good standing place.

Taittiriya Upanishad Dialogue of philosophical and spiritual wisdom; part of the Yajur Veda. (The *Upanishads* contain the essence of the *Vedas* in an anthology of discourses.)

tapasya Literally: To burn it, produced by heat; steadfast disciplines; austerities and penances, the 'fire' of which destroys impurities of the mind.

vasanas tendancies; present knowledge derived from memory.

Vedas Literally: true knowledge; science; ancient sacred texts.

VIDYA VĀCASPATI 'Lord of Learning'.

VIRUKTA SIROMANI 'He who has accomplished the Supreme Renunciation'.

Vishnu (Visnu) Personification of God as the Preserver and Sustainer of goodness and virtue; the Omnipotent, Omniscient, Omnipresent

vishuddha Implying the quality of complete purification; removal of all doubt and error (throat chakra).

Yogi (Yogin) King, master of the yoga system.

Yogiraj King of yogis.

yuga Age, era, astronomical cycle of years. There are four yugas:
1. satya – age of truth; golden age
2. treta – age of triads; silver age
3. dvapara – age of twilight
4. kali – age of darkness

BOOKS OF RELATED INTEREST FROM NAB

BETWEEN EAST AND WEST: From Singularity to Community—*Luce Irigaray*
A leading philosopher steeped in the Western tradition explores ancient Eastern disciplines, meditating on what it means to learn to breathe: the result is a powerful challenge to discover the relevance of indigenous Asian philosophy to our lives. According to Luce Irigaray, yogic tradition can provide a vital link between the present and eternity, allowing us to reexamine and reenvision the patriarchal traditions of the West.

ISBN: 978-81-7822-215-8

DIALOGUES ON REALITY: An Exploration into the Nature of Our Ultimate Identity—*Robert Powell*
Dialogues on Reality leads us to genuine self-enquiry, stimulates to deeper self-examination and takes us beyond the realm of ego. The ego, a composite of falseness and the source of all trouble, is destroyer of freedom of consciousness. Besides, the book discusses I-Principle as well as *Maya* Principle and Consciousness and a number of other related themes on the subject-matter.

ISBN: 978-81-7822-140-3

ENCOUNTERS WITH INFINITY: A Metamathematical Dissertation—*Michael Van Laanen*
The original title of this manuscript was *Pages-A Voyage to Infinity*. It's kinda like Walt Whitman's *Leaves of Grass,* Like a collection of poems with an underlying mystical theme, this dissertation is a kaleidoscope puzzle of images and thoughts and concepts and ideas taken from mysticism, science, logic, and mathematics. The end result, as the puzzle pieces are linked together, is a new portrait of Number.

ISBN: 978-81-7822-185-4

HOPE FOR A BETTER WORLD!: The Small Communities Solution—*J. Donald Walters*
A thesis, supported by practical wisdom, on how to create a better life on earth. For those who dream of seeing true peace on earth someday, *Hope for a Better World!* offers a convincing blueprint. In a progressive series of deeply insightful analyses, J. Donald Walters examines why certain societies of the past failed, and how others in future might succeed.

ISBN: 978-81-7822-141-0

THE SUPREME YOGA: A new translation of the Yoga Vāsiṣṭha Vol. I—*Swami Venkatesananda*
The Supreme Yoga presented as a rosary of daily thoughts for contemplation throughout the year, this book offers a comprehensive spirituality for creative living and innerfulfilment. Its romanised text, is a translation into English of this complete work. This book brings this storehouse of wisdom to our world and makes the philosophy comprehensible to scholars and common people alike.

ISBN: 978-81-7822-260-8

THE QUIET MIND: A Journey through Space and Mind—*John E. Coleman*
Since this book was originally published, there seems to have been a flood tide of interest in "the search." *The Quiet Mind* remains a testament to this search, and offers the hope and the inspiration that the goal can be reached. It expands on the original edition with the addition of a postscript, which tells the story of the author's experience since the events in the book, and describes how the tools for finding a "quiet mind" have spread to the West since the first edition.

ISBN: 978-81-7822-176-2

THE ART OF BLISSFUL LIVING: Spiritual laws of vedic philosophy—*Prof. B.B. Puri*
Various techniques of the art of blissful living by positive thoughts, love gratitude and compassion towards everyone and acceptance of whatever life offers, Yoga, meditation, healthy diet, rich in fruits and vegetables (Satvik Diet) as described in our Vedic Philosophy have been well illustrated.

ISBN: 978-81-7822-307-0

THE ART OF GETTING WELL: A Five-Step Plan for Maximizing Health When You Have A Chronic Illness—*David Spero*
The Art of Getting Well emphassises awareness and balance. This practical and profound guide, provides a host of skills that will help you develop your art and get well not just through will power and following orders but also by improving the quality of life.

ISBN: 978-81-7822-288-2

THE PHILOSOPHY OF SELF-REALISATION OF SWAMI YOGESHWARANANDA SARASWATI: —*Dr. Inder Bhan Bhasin*
The book makes some sensational departures from established concepts of Sāmkhya and Yoga philosophies in spite of being a staunch follower of these systems.

ISBN: 978-81-7822-311-7